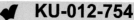

# Legend

| | | | |
|---|---|---|---|
| ← - - - - - | Walk route | P | Car park |
| •••••••• | Optional walk route | ≈≈≈ | Cliff |
| - - - - - - | Adjoining footpath | | Rock outcrop |
| — · — · — | County boundary | | Beach |
| ☀ | Viewpoint | ♣ ♧ | Woodland |
| ▲ 392 | Spot height | | Parkland |
| 🗾 | Built-up area | † | Church, cathedral, chapel |
| ● | Place of interest | WC | Toilet |
| △ | Steep section | 🎍 | Picnic area |

# London locator map

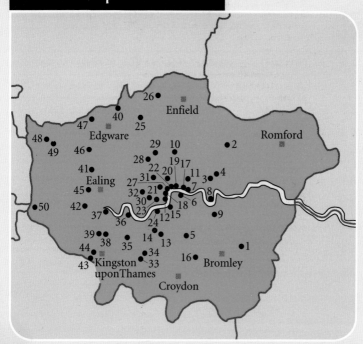

26● Enfield

40 ●
47 ● 25 ●
Edgware
48 ● 29 ● 10 ● ●2 Romford
49 46 ●
41 ● 28 ● 19 17
22 20 11
Ealing 31 ● 7 3 ●4
45 ● 27 ● 21 8
32 30 18 6
42 ● 23 12 15 ●9
37 ● 24
36
39 ● 14 13 ●5
38 35 34 16● Bromley ●1
44 43 ● Kingston 33
uponThames
Croydon

●50

Contents

Contents

**Rating:** Each walk is rated for its relative difficulty compared to the other walks in this book. Walks marked 🚶🚶🚶 are likely to be shorter and easier with little total ascent. The hardest walks are marked 🚶🚶🚶 .

**Walking in Safety:** For advice and safety tips ➤ 128.

# Introducing London

London's diversity makes it one of the world's greatest capitals and a city simply made for walking. The major artery is the River Thames, which once provided its most convenient form of transport – witness the many palaces built near the river's banks. Today, the Thames remains one of the best places from which to see the dynamic skyline, where classical and modern architecture sit side by side. London is a capital with green lungs, for its Royal Parks are never far away. At its heart is an exhilarating mass of streets, alleys and lanes, but if you go off the beaten track then you'll find plenty of quiet corners.

The 72 mile (116km) Thames Path, which follows the route of the river and passes many riverside pubs, is a natural wildlife highway. Others paths include the 150 mile (241km) London Loop, which will eventually encircle the capital and become the walker's equivalent to the M25, and its sibling, the circular Capital Ring. In all, there are thousands of miles of footpaths, pavements and tow paths to explore, connecting a network of capillaries that encompass London . While some of the walks may seem short in length, there are so many interesting facets to investigate that they could easily take at least double the estimated time.

Outside the central region is a surprising wealth of nature reserves, wetland areas and places of historical interest that have much to offer the walker. In the east are canals, once dumping grounds for industrial waste, but now restored and rejuvenated channels where wildlife thrives. South London's commons form the basis of some varied walks. In the north you'll find rural Totteridge, with its hay meadows and butterflies, and the ancient woods of Highgate. There are hills that offer some fine views over the city too, including Primrose Hill in the north, and Horsenden Hill and Harrow on the Hill in the west. Also in this area are the woods near Ruislip Lido and the delightful Harmondsworth Moor.

There is something for everyone here. Walk along the disused railway track from Finsbury Park to discover an enchanting green corridor running through the urban landscape; in Trent Country Park enjoy the woodland scenery surrounding a mansion that once held lavish society parties; or in Bushy Park follow the path that was declared a public right of way by a local cobbler. The Osterley and Brent River Valley walks show how the

### PUBLIC TRANSPORT  ⓘ

London has an excellent public transport system, giving easy access to most of these walks. The London Underground, Docklands Light Railway, Tramlink and local rail and bus networks are all fully integrated and run from early in the morning until late at night. Congestion charging for motorists entering central London makes car travel unattractive, though you may find that it is the only realistic way of accessing some of the outlying country parks. For London travel information call 020 7222 1234.

Industrial Revolution improved transportation, passing some of Brunel's finest engineering feats.

London has more than its fair share of museums – in fact, in excess of 300. Some of the most architecturally impressive are in South Kensington, dating back to the Great Exhibition of 1851, organised by Prince Albert. Charles Dickens, who thought nothing of walking 20 miles (32km) in a day, put his gift of observation to good use in his novels which depicted city life – his words may echo off the walls as you walk through the Inns of Court. Stroll around Wanstead Park, as Elizabeth I once did, or trace the route of the Great Fire of London and discover who benefited from the disaster. You might peep into the Botanical Gardens in Kew from the Thames Path, or even follow in the footsteps of the fictional James Bond through Mayfair.

Whichever you choose, there is no other place like London for diverse scenery. If you want to get away from the usual tourist attractions and discover the best that London has to offer on foot, fasten your laces – now.

## Using this Book

### Information panels
An information panel for each walk shows its relative difficulty (➤ 5), the distance and total amount of ascent. An indication of the gradients you will encounter is shown by the rating ▲▲▲ (no steep slopes) to ▲▲▲ (several very steep slopes).

### Maps
There are 30 maps, covering 40 of the walks. Some walks have a suggested option in the same area. The information panel for these walks will tell you how much extra walking is involved. On short-cut suggestions the panel will tell you the total distance if you set out from the start of the main walk. Where an option returns to the same point on the main walk, just the distance of the loop is given. Where an option leaves the main walk at one point and returns to it at another, then the distance shown is for the whole walk. The minimum time suggested is for reasonably fit walkers and doesn't allow for stops. Each walk has a suggested map. Laminated aqua3 maps are longer lasting and water resistant.

### Start Points
Most walks in this guide give a tube or rail station as the starting point. Others have a six-figure grid reference prefixed by two letters indicating which 100km square of the National Grid it refers to. You'll find more information on grid references on most Ordnance Survey maps.

### Dogs
We have tried to give dog owners useful advice about how dog friendly each walk is. Please respect other countryside users. Keep your dog under control, especially around livestock, and obey local bylaws and other dog control notices.

### Car Parking
Most of the walks in central London begin and end at a station. Getting to these points by car is not advised. Where access by car is more practical, a public car park has been suggested. Please be considerate when you leave your car.

**Walk 1**

# Daylight Saving in Chislehurst

*The inventor of British Summer Time, Napoleon III and Zulus – Chislehurst has connections with all three.*

| | |
|---|---|
| •DISTANCE• | 3½ miles (5.7km) |
| •MINIMUM TIME• | 2hrs |
| •ASCENT / GRADIENT• | 98ft (30m) ▲▲ ▲▲ ▲▲ |
| •LEVEL OF DIFFICULTY• | 🚶🚶 🚶🚶 🚶 |
| •PATHS• | Footpaths, field edges and bridle paths |
| •LANDSCAPE• | Common and woodland |
| •SUGGESTED MAP• | aqua3 OS Explorer 162 Greenwich & Gravesend |
| •START / FINISH• | Grid reference: TQ 439708; Chislehurst rail 1 mile (1.6km) |
| •DOG FRIENDLINESS• | On lead near Hawkwood Estate as could be sheep in fields |
| •PARKING• | Pay-and-display in High Street (or Queen's Head for patrons) |
| •PUBLIC TOILETS• | None on route |

## BACKGROUND TO THE WALK

Chislehurst is a delightful mixture of the quaint and the historic. Although the town is just 3 miles (4.8km) from the South Circular, you could be forgiven for thinking that you were in the heart of the countryside during much of this walk.

### Willett's Daylight Saving

The inventor of British Summer Time lived in Chislehurst. William Willett was a builder by trade. On this walk you will pass his house, Cedars, which he built himself. It was while out riding in nearby Petts Wood one day that he was inspired by an idea to increase the hours of light in the day 'to improve health and happiness'. He soon became obsessed with the concept. In 1907 he circulated a pamphlet around Parliament and town councils, which argued that the many hours of light wasted while people slept in the mornings should be transferred to the evenings. Although it was met with considerable opposition, a Daylight Saving Bill was introduced in 1909. However, it would take another seven years to pass.

Had it not been for the First World War, Willett's idea may have remained on the shelf but, in 1916, a committee was set up to investigate ways of saving fuel. Consequently Willett's suggestion was given serious consideration. Indeed, it was introduced as a wartime economy measure in many countries on both sides. Sadly, William Willett never lived to see his scheme put into effect as he died in 1915. However, his summer-time legacy lives on and today, Britain keeps Greenwich Mean Time (GMT) in winter and British Summer Time (BST) in summer, (for more about GMT ▶ Walk 8).

### The French Connection

Another former Chislehurst resident played an historic role in world affairs, and the course of history in the 20th century would have been very different had Napoleon III's son, Eugene, the French Prince Imperial, married Beatrice, the daughter of Queen Victoria. The two had become friends but he chose an army career. After training at Woolwich Barracks he went to war in South Africa to fight against the Zulus – he died, it is said, from one of 17 spear wounds to his body. The golf clubhouse near the beginning of the walk was once home to Napoleon III and his wife, Eugenie. Nathaniel Strode, a local man, lent them the building, which was then a private house, when they were exiled from France in 1871. When Napoleon III died in 1873 his body was laid to rest in a chapel at the side of St Mary's Church, before being buried at Farnborough, Hampshire.

# Walk 1 Directions

① Walk down **Chislehurst High Street**, past **Prick End Pond**, cross the road and turn right into **Prince Imperial Road**. Follow this as it passes a row of large houses and, 50yds (46m) further on, the **Methodist church**. Where the houses end, take the bridle path to the right, running through the trees parallel to the road. When you cross **Wilderness Road** look left to see the memorial to Eugene, the French Prince Imperial.

② Just past the golf clubhouse is William Willett's **Cedars** (built in 1893), identified by a blue plaque. Cross the road and walk up **Watts Lane** to the left of the cricket

**Walk 1**

ground. About 150yds (137m) further on, after a field, is a crossroads. In a few paces take the narrow, tarmac path towards **St Nicholas Church**. Just before the trees turn sharp right and follow a path to the right of the church, leaving by the lychgate.

---

**WHAT TO LOOK FOR** ⓘ

As you walk along the tarmac path towards St Nicholas Church notice the sunken area of grass to the left. This is the remains of a **cockpit**, used for cock fighting – a once-popular sport that was eventually banned in England in 1834.

---

③ Walk down **Hawkwood Lane** to the left of the **Tiger's Head** pub. After **St Mary's Church** and **Coopers School** the road bends to the left and joins **Botany Bay Lane**. Continue ahead but, when you see a National Trust sign, take the footpath on the left into the **Hawkwood Estate**, keeping to the right of the central fence. The path descends through woodland and along a boardwalk that skirts the edge of a pond. It then climbs steadily alongside a field (which may contain sheep). At the top is a fine view of Petts Wood.

---

**WHERE TO EAT AND DRINK** ⓘ

The **Queen's Head** at the start of the walk serves a range of snacks, jacket potatoes and salads, but for a wider choice of food, hand pulled ales and wine, try the **Tiger's Head** half-way along the walk. The dishes are written on chalkboards and fresh fish is a speciality. Dogs are allowed in the patio area.

---

④ At a T-junction turn left and follow the bridle path through the wood until you reach **St Paul's Cray Road**. Cross the road, turn left and take the path running parallel to the road. After 500yds (457m) the path

---

**WHILE YOU'RE THERE** ⓘ

**Chislehurst Caves** (near the railway station) runs lamp-lit tours of a labyrinth of tunnels, spanning more than 20 miles (32km), that were carved from the rocks 8,000 years ago. They have been a druidical base and a wartime air-raid shelter. During the First World War they were used as an ammunition depot. The caves have also served as a film location for *Doctor Who* and legendary rock guitarist, Jimi Hendrix, played to 3,000 fans here in 1967.

---

emerges from the woodland by **Graham Chiesman House**. Note the village sign depicting Elizabeth I knighting Thomas Walsingham in 1597. Continue to the war memorial by the crossroads. Cross **Bromley Lane**.

⑤ A few paces further, take a footpath on the left, just before **Kemnal Road**. Continue along a wide track through the common (you can follow the pavement if this section is muddy). After a pond on the right, cross the road and follow a footpath diagonally opposite through some trees. Continue along **Chislehurst High Street**, back to the start.

# Wanstead and its Royal Connections

*Through Wanstead Park, where Robert Dudley, the Earl of Leicester, entertained Elizabeth I.*

| | |
|---:|:---|
| •DISTANCE• | 4¾ miles (7.7km) |
| •MINIMUM TIME• | 2hrs 30min |
| •ASCENT / GRADIENT• | Negligible |
| •LEVEL OF DIFFICULTY• | |
| •PATHS• | Mainly lakeside tracks that can get muddy |
| •LANDSCAPE• | Ornamental lake and parkland |
| •SUGGESTED MAP• | aqua3 OS Explorer 174 Epping Forest & Lee Valley |
| •START / FINISH• | Grid reference TQ 406882; Wanstead tube |
| •DOG FRIENDLINESS• | Keep on lead on roads to park |
| •PUBLIC TOILETS• | By Temple |

## BACKGROUND TO THE WALK

The surprising thing about Wanstead Park in east London is that, despite its close proximity to the North Circular road, the distant hum of traffic is really only noticeable from the northern side of the park. This is a lovely walk, enchanting even, for it traces the outline of the ornamental waters and its Grotto and Temple as well as Florrie's Hill. No wonder Elizabeth I kept returning.

### An Estate Like No Other

Wanstead has been associated with royalty ever since 1553 when Queen Mary, a Catholic, broke her journey here from Norwich to meet her sister, Princess Elizabeth, a Protestant, who rode out to Wanstead accompanied by hundreds of knights on horseback. The estate had belonged to Sir Giles Heron but, because he would not denounce his Catholic beliefs, Henry VIII (the girls' father) took it from him. After Mary's death, Elizabeth became Queen – she was just 25 years old. The estate at Wanstead then belonged to Robert Dudley, the Earl of Leicester, who had enlarged and improved the mansion. The two became very close and Dudley held some extremely lavish parties for his royal guest. In 1578 Elizabeth stayed in Wanstead for five days and no doubt would have spent some time walking in the wonderful grounds.

### Highs and Lows

When Queen Elizabeth died, James I succeeded her. In 1607 he spent the autumn in Wanstead. The manor was later sold to Sir James Mildmay. Unfortunately, as Mildmay was one of the judges at the trial of Charles I, which led to Charles' execution, the manor was taken from the family after the restoration and handed to the Crown. In 1667 Sir Josiah Child (whose family were the first private bankers in England) bought the manor and made huge improvements. Later, his son, Sir Richard, replaced the manor house and landscaped the gardens. Constructed using Portland stone, the front of the new mansion had a portico of six Corinthian columns. The building was considered one of the finest in the country, even rivalling Blenheim Palace. The Grotto was erected and the ornamental waters and lakes were also designed at this time. But why, you might ask, is there no mansion today? The blame lies chiefly with Catherine Tilney-Long, who inherited the extremely valuable property in 1794. Despite no shortage of admiring males, she married a gambling man, who took just ten years to blow her entire fortune. To pay off her husband's debts Catherine auctioned the contents of the house and, because a buyer could not be found for the house itself, the magnificent property was pulled down and sold in separate lots. Fortunately for us, despite this sad tale of decline, the wonderful grounds can still be enjoyed.

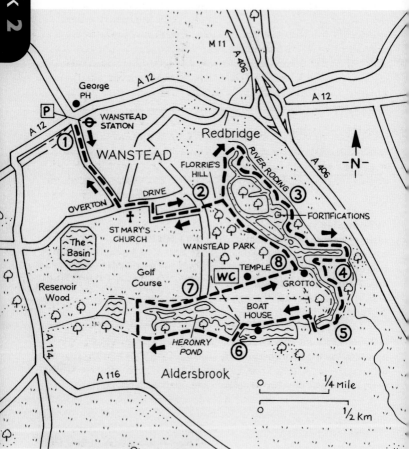

# Walk 2 Directions

① Turn left outside **Wanstead tube** into **The Green**, which becomes **St Mary's Avenue**. At the end cross the road into **Overton Drive**, which runs to the left of **St Mary's Church**. After the Bowls and Golf Club turn right, into **The Warren**

**Drive**. (The building on the right, before the road bends, was once the stable block and coach house to Wanstead House.)

② At the T-junction turn left and, almost immediately, enter **Wanstead Park** through the gate opposite. Continue ahead downhill (**Florrie's Hill**) to reach the

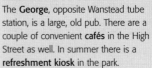

Walk 2

ornamental water. Follow the path to the left of the water and continue ahead as it runs to the right of the **River Roding**.

③ After another ¼ mile (400m) the path swings sharply to the left round an area known as the **Fortifications**, once a group of eight islands used for storing ammunition for duck-shooting and now a bird sanctuary. Soon after this the path traces the outline of a section of the water shaped like a finger. To your left are the steep banks of the **River Roding**.

④ At a meeting of paths turn right to continue alongside the water. When the path bends to the left, you will see the **Grotto** ahead.

⑤ At the T-junction turn right. At the end of the water turn right again, to cross a footbridge; then take the left-hand fork towards a field. At a crossing of paths keep ahead until you reach a boathouse. Turn left here and go out through the gate.

⑥ Immediately turn right to pick up a path leading to **Heronry Pond**, which narrows and passes over a mound. At a crossing of paths turn

---

### WHERE TO EAT AND DRINK ⓘ
The **George**, opposite Wanstead tube station, is a large, old pub. There are a couple of convenient **cafés** in the High Street as well. In summer there is a **refreshment kiosk** in the park.

---

right and keep ahead across the grass. At the next junction turn sharp right, towards the trees.

⑦ The path weaves around the pond to reach a metal gate. Go through this and take a left-hand fork to join a wide, grassy track lined with sweet chestnut trees. At the front of the Temple take the well-defined path on your right. A few paces further on turn left and continue on this path alongside the **Temple**. Keep ahead, ignoring the next path on the right.

---

### WHAT TO LOOK FOR ⓘ
Spare a moment to gaze at the fairytale **Grotto**, which was overlooked when Wanstead House was pulled down. Now a Grade II listed building, it was encrusted with shells, stalactites, crystals and pebbles, many of which were found in the lake after a fire damaged the Grotto in 1884. The chamber had a domed roof and a stained glass window and it was accessible by a set of steps from the lake.

---

### WHILE YOU'RE THERE ⓘ
**St Mary's Church** in Overton Drive is where Elizabeth I worshipped during her many visits to Wanstead. Grecian in style and cased with white Portland stone, it has four imposing columns. The church was designed by Thomas Hardwick, who was also associated with the building of Somerset House. You'll find a monument to the memory of Sir Josiah Child in the chancel.

---

⑧ When you reach the metal enclosure that surrounds the Grotto turn sharp left, as if you are going back on yourself, but, a few paces further on, take a footpath that veers right and hugs the water's edge before joining another, wider path. Turn next left up **Florrie's Hill** to retrace your steps back to **Wanstead tube**.

# Three Mills and the Canals

*Discover the history of the East End waterways on this tow path walk.*

| | |
|---|---|
| **•DISTANCE•** | 4¼ miles (6.8km) |
| **•MINIMUM TIME•** | 2hrs 30min |
| **•ASCENT / GRADIENT•** | Negligible |
| **•LEVEL OF DIFFICULTY•** | |
| **•PATHS•** | Gravel, tarmac and tow paths |
| **•LANDSCAPE•** | Mainly canalside industry and housing |
| **•SUGGESTED MAP•** | aqua3 OS Explorers 162 Greenwich & Gravesend; 173 London North |
| **•START / FINISH•** | TQ 383828; near Bromley-by-Bow tube (on Explorer 173) |
| **•DOG FRIENDLINESS•** | No particular problems |
| **•PARKING•** | Tesco car park, Three Mill Lane; Bromley-by-Bow tube ¼ mile (400m) |
| **•PUBLIC TOILETS•** | At car park |

## BACKGROUND TO THE WALK

In the mid 19th century the banks of the River Lea were lined with flourishing industries. At that time, because it was deemed to be outside the City of London with its stringent pollution regulations, the water and surrounding air quality were dangerously poor. Since the demise of canal transport, this area, which is just a few steps away from hectic everyday life, has been transformed into a clean, peaceful haven for both walkers and wildlife.

### Life Along the Lea

In the 14th century Edward III instigated a policy to encourage commercial expansion, which led to the manufacture of gunpowder, paper, soap, flour and porcelain along the Lea. These were vibrant times, but it wasn't until the 1700s that work was carried out on the meandering river to construct straight channels and build locks so that freight could be transported more easily. Some parts of east London were more significant than others in the development of the chemical industry. West Ham, for example, was just outside the jurisdiction of the Metropolitan Buildings Act of 1844 that protected the City from anti-social trades such as oil-burning and varnish making. Industry developed in Bromley-by-Bow because there was lots of cheap land and no building restrictions.

### The Demise of the Waterways

As the Industrial Revolution progressed in the 19th century, the River Lea became an enormous health hazard. The factories along its banks produced a great deal of waste – the river was, in effect, used as a dumping ground for chemical and pharmaceutical waste. Looking at the scene before you today, it's not easy to picture a skyline of mass industrialism. Warehouses, cranes and gas works were here, against a backdrop of smoggy, smelly air. But, together with the noise of the powerful machinery, this would have been a way of life for many workers. For more than half of the 20th century barges still brought raw materials to the factories from London Docks, taking away the finished goods. Today, however, you're more likely to see a heron than a vessel on this stretch of the river.

# Walk 3 Directions

① From the Tesco supermarket car park in **Three Mills Lane** take the footpath to the left of an iron bridge marked 'Lee Navigation Tow Path' and 'Bow Flyover'. Continue walking ahead with the river to your right-hand side and you will shortly see the formidable volume of traffic coming into view, going across the Bow Flyover.

② Where the path ends walk up the ramp on your left, leading to the **A12**. Turn right, cross the **A11** ahead of you and turn right at the railings. Now walk down the slope and across a bridge to rejoin the tow path, with the river now to your left. Notice the brickwork of the old Bryant & May **match factory** ahead to your left. The path swings right, away from the traffic. Ignore the Greenway sign on the right (as this will be covered in the extension in Walk 4) and pass under two pipes that are part of the old Victorian sewer. Cross a bridge and continue along the **River Lea**, past the **Old Ford Lock**.

③ Just before the next bridge ahead, the **Hertford Union Canal** emerges and joins at a right angle on the left. Cross the bridge and turn left down a slope to join this canal along a gravel path. Pass **Bottom Lock**, **Middle Lock** and, further on, **Top Lock**. Once past the cottages of Top Lock, **Victoria Park** is visible on the right. Continue along this long, straight, paved path until you pass under **Three Colts Bridge**, a metal gate, two further bridges and another metal gate.

> **WHERE TO EAT AND DRINK** ⓘ
>
> At the footbridge joining the Regent's Canal is Bow Wharf where you'll find the **Fat Cat Café and Bar**. A converted builders' yard, it has outside, daytime seating and a wooden interior with Chesterfield sofas. A good selection of wines, and beers include IPA and Spitfire.

④ Cross a footbridge at this T-junction of the waterways to pick up the southern section of the **Regent's Canal**, which was opened in 1820 and used by horse-drawn barges to haul coal through London. Continue along the canal, towards the blinking light of Canary Wharf. Pass under a railway bridge, **Mile End Lock**, two more bridges and **Jonson Lock**. Pass a red brick chimney, which is a sewer

> **WHILE YOU'RE THERE**
>
> The **Ragged School Museum** in Copperfield Road was one of 148 schools set up by Dr Barnardo to educate poor children in London. The museum highlights the history of the East End, with a Victorian schoolroom taster session for children.

ventilation shaft, and walk under a railway bridge. Continue past **Salmon Lock** and notice the viaduct ahead. After walking under **Commercial Road Bridge**, turn left and follow the steps to the road.

⑤ Turn right along **Commercial Road** and pass **Limehouse Library** and a small park on the right. Ignore the first gate on the right and instead pass over a bridge and take the steps on the right-hand side that lead down to the canal. Turn right and follow the tow path of the canal, the **Limehouse Cut**, with the water on your left. A few paces further on pass under the **A13**. Follow the tarmac path under three more bridges until it leads on to the **A102**. Walk along the pavement for 50yds (46m) and cross the road using the underpass ahead of you.

⑥ Turn right, walking with the flow of traffic, and take the first road on the left to pick up the canal path at **Bow Locks**. Walk over the concrete footbridge and under two bridges. Continue ahead towards the **Mill House**. Turn left over the bridge back to the start.

> **WHAT TO LOOK FOR** ⓘ
>
> A Swedish manufacturer of matchsticks sold the British patent to Mr Bryant and Mr May who, in 1855, leased the **factory**, Bryant & May. A medical condition called 'phossy jaw' was common among workers and was often fatal. The fumes from the yellow phosphorous in the head of the match caused the jawbone to rot away – the smell from the diseased bone was apparently horrendous. In 1911 a new factory was built on the site; the remains have been converted into luxury flats.

# Three Mills – Take Two

*A look at the island's 'Cathedral of Sewage' and its industrial past.*
**See map and information panel for Walk 3**

Walk 4

| | |
|---|---|
| •DISTANCE• | 1½ miles (2.4km) |
| •MINIMUM TIME• | 1hr |
| •ASCENT / GRADIENT• | Negligible |
| •LEVEL OF DIFFICULTY• | |

## Walk 4 Directions
(Walk 3 option)

This additional trail along the waterways contrasts the industrial past of Three Mills with its present-day role as a base for music, film and television studios.

At Point ① on Walk 3 cross the **iron bridge** and continue along the cobbled road. Turn right at the gates to **Three Mills Film Studios**, along a path between the mill buildings. Follow this **Long Wall Path** and cross a footbridge over the **Prescott Channel**. At the end of the bridge is an empty field where the house and gardens of Channel 4's *Big Brother* stood. In its heyday the **House Mill**, the largest tidal mill in the country, supplied flour to London bakers. It has a small museum and a scale model showing how the mill once operated.

Follow the path that bends to the left. Soon **Channelsea Island** appears on the right, flanked by reeds. This was once home to a factory that supplied rockets during the Napoleonic Wars. Where the path forks, take the higher path on the left alongside the **Abbey Mills Pumping Station**, Point Ⓐ.

During a 20-year span in the mid-1800s, cholera outbreaks claimed the lives of nearly 30,000 Londoners. The answer lay in effectively removing sewage from the water supply. In 1860 the beautiful Abbey Mills Pumping Station was built to pump raw sewage to treatment works away from the city. The Thames is now one of the cleanest metropolitan rivers in the world.

At a big piece of redundant machinery shaped like a giant snail, turn left along the Greenway, a huge set of Victorian pipes built to take sewage out of London. Continue ahead through a gate at **Stratford High Street**, Point Ⓑ.

The building opposite, **Watton House**, once belonged to Yardley Cosmetics. Turn left and walk along the **High Street**, then cross **Abbey Lane** and take the path on the left, signposted to Three Mills. Cross the bridge over **Prescott Channel** and enter **Three Mills Green**, Point Ⓒ. Climb up the hill for a glimpse across the island. Now descend the steps and turn right. Take the left-hand fork and go through a gate. Turn left, cross the road and turn right at the building, following the path past the **Mill House** and back to the car park.

**Walk 5**

# Due South for an Exploration of Dulwich

*Through the leafy lanes and woods of Dulwich, where explorer Ernest Shackleton went to college.*

| | |
|---|---|
| •DISTANCE• | 3½ miles (5.7km) |
| •MINIMUM TIME• | 1hr 30min |
| •ASCENT / GRADIENT• | 164ft (50m) ▲▲▲ |
| •LEVEL OF DIFFICULTY• | 🚶🚶 🚶🚶 🚶 |
| •PATHS• | Tarmac paths and some woodland tracks |
| •LANDSCAPE• | Village of Dulwich and its woodlands |
| •SUGGESTED MAP• | aqua3 OS Explorer 161 London South |
| •START / FINISH• | Grid reference: TQ 328731; West Dulwich rail |
| •DOG FRIENDLINESS• | Keep on lead near lake |
| •PARKING• | Some in roads near station |
| •PUBLIC TOILETS• | None on route |

## Walk 5 Directions

From **West Dulwich Station** turn right along **Thurlow Park Road**, cross the road and turn right, just after passing the playing fields, into **College Road**.

Dulwich is one of London's oldest recorded villages – it only became a part of London when the city was expanded administratively. A few minutes from the South Circular, Dulwich is still a world apart from the capital. While the famed Dulwich College may be its centrepiece, this is only the tip of the iceberg, for there are some quaint medieval lanes to explore and Dulwich Woods, not to mention the village itself and its many restaurants.

On the right the attractive buildings of **Dulwich College** are made of a deep-red brick that resembles terracotta. The college was built in

1618 to educate poor boys. Edward Alleyn, a prominent actor at the time and owner of two Bankside playhouses, financed the project. Even today, former pupils are known as 'Old Alleynians'.

> **WHAT TO LOOK FOR**
> If you go down to Sydenham Woods in spring, you will probably notice the unmistakable odour of **ramsons**, also known as wild garlic. The plant is part of the lily family and its bright green leaves are shaped like spears. The long stalks resemble stars and are also used for medicinal purposes.

Ernest Shackleton (1874–1922) was educated at Dulwich College for three years. As his family lived in nearby Sydenham he was a day pupil, but he left, aged 16, to join the Merchant Navy. Ten years later he joined the 1901–4 British expedition to the South Pole, led by Captain Scott. At the age of 33, while leading his own gruelling expedition, he came within 97 miles

(156km) of the South Pole. Despite this failure, it was Shackleton's dogged and inspirational leadership which won him respect. Determined not to repeat Scott's tragic mistakes, he led his team safely out of the Antarctic with no loss of life.

Follow the road past the **toll gate**, which dates from 1789 and has a board indicating that the pre- decimalisation amount payable for cars to pass here was 6*d* (2½ new pence). You'll have to pay somewhat more for that privilege now, though it's free for pedestrians. This is the last toll gate in use in London. It was erected by a farmer who once rented the surrounding fields from Dulwich College, and they continued the tradition after his death. After a further 550 yds (503m) find a path on your left, practically opposite Sydenham Hill Station. Walk through the kissing gate and along **Low Cross Wood Lane**, which descends quite steeply to reach another gate. Opposite this is an Italianate building, the **Dulwich Wood House** (now converted into a pub).

Turn left into **Crescent Wood Road** and, opposite a block of flats, go through another kissing gate into **Sydenham Woods**, a nature reserve managed by the London Wildlife Trust. Walk down the slope and turn right down the steps. Follow the track and, where another one

meets it, bear to the right of a wooden marker, to the left of which are some ruins. Next bear left and, a few steps further on, you will pass a pond. Turn right to join a long path that follows the trackbed of an old railway. (If you'd like to see the remains of the old railway tunnel, turn left here and then retrace your steps.) Where the path ends go up some steps on the left and bear right to follow a row of wooden posts. There are some good views across London from here. Go through a kissing gate and continue ahead, ignoring the bridge on your right, along the wide **Cox's Walk**, a path that passes the golf course.

---

### WHERE TO EAT AND DRINK ⓘ

The **Crown and Greyhound** in Dulwich village is a pub of monstrous proportions but it has a friendly, unassuming air. One of the bars, serving Old Speckled Hen, Tetley's and Young's, contains Victorian prints, gas lamps and an ornate ceiling. The former billiards room is now a self-service restaurant with wooden kitchen tables. The large portions of home-made food include a vegetarian option.

---

At the end turn left, along **Dulwich Common Road**. After 440yds (402m) turn right into **Dulwich Park**. Take the wide tarmac path on the left, past the park lodge. Where some paths meet take the central path, then bear right, with the lake on your right. A few paces beyond a bronze statue, cross the bridge over the lake, bear right and take the path to the park gates, towards a white building in **College Road**.

Turn left and cross the road to visit the **Dulwich Picture Gallery**. Continue along this road. At **Dulwich Common** turn right to retrace your steps back to **West Dulwich Station**.

---

### WHILE YOU'RE THERE ⓘ

If you'd like to visit England's oldest public picture gallery, head for **Dulwich Picture Gallery** in College Road. It actually dates from 1626 but was later re-designed by John Soane and has a magnificent collection of Old Masters and 18th-century paintings.

**Walk 6**

# Bargains in Borough

*An urban walk south of the river to two of London's famous markets.*

| | |
|---|---|
| •DISTANCE• | 5½ miles (8.8km) |
| •MINIMUM TIME• | 3hrs |
| •ASCENT / GRADIENT• | Negligible ▲▲ ▲ ▲ |
| •LEVEL OF DIFFICULTY• | 👥 👥 👥 |
| •PATHS• | Mainly paved |
| •LANDSCAPE• | Urban with views over Docklands |
| •SUGGESTED MAP• | aqua3 OS Explorer 173 London North |
| •START• | Grid reference: TQ 323797; Borough tube |
| •FINISH• | Grid reference: TQ 352979; Rotherhithe tube |
| •DOG FRIENDLINESS• | On lead except in Russia Dock Woodland |
| •PUBLIC TOILETS• | Southwark Park |

## BACKGROUND TO THE WALK

Historically, Borough, Bermondsey and Rotherhithe were quite poor areas. Until a few years ago, very few people wanted to live in Bermondsey and in particular, Rotherhithe but, since the expansion of Canary Wharf and the addition of new transport links, it has been drawing more interest. To experience the specialist food and antiques markets here you will have to start this walk early – but early birds will be rewarded.

In the past, writers have been less than flattering about Rotherhithe, or Redriff as it was called during the time Samuel Pepys was writing his diaries (part of the route is along Redriff Road). In *Our Mutual Friend* (1864–5), Dickens writes of Rotherhithe, ' …down by where accumulated scum of humanity seems to be washed from higher grounds like so much moral sewage…'. The early part of Moll Flander's career as a prostitute, according to the author Daniel Defoe, was also spent in Redriff; it was certainly popular with sailors and renowned at the time for its many pubs. As in Docklands, developers have created some expensive properties for those after a spot of lofty living but the skyline was very different 100 years ago. The land was marshy and liable to flooding. Behind the riverside houses were farms and market gardens; the only things to look up to were church spires. Southwark Park now stands on the site of some of these market gardens. Although the area has more than its fair share of social housing (many homes have been bought in 'Right to Buy' schemes), the markets have a richness unique to south London and the East End.

Borough Market is the last remaining early morning wholesale fruit and vegetable market in central London, where traders are joined on Fridays and Saturdays by a variety of specialist food retailers. Expect to see stalls selling anything from French cheeses and Cumbrian wild boar meat to barbecued burgers and organic vegetables, in an atmosphere more akin to a Dickens' novel. If you need proof, then enter from Bedale Street and witness the scene beneath the market's Victorian, cast-iron canopy.

Bermondsey Antiques Market is altogether different. For a start, the serious dealers have usually completed their trading by 4AM, when most of us are still asleep and before even the birds start searching for worms. It's an experience though, trying to find a bargain that would fare well on the *Antiques Road Show*. There are plenty of warehouses, such as Aladdin's Cave in Long Lane, selling paintings, china, furniture and jewellery.

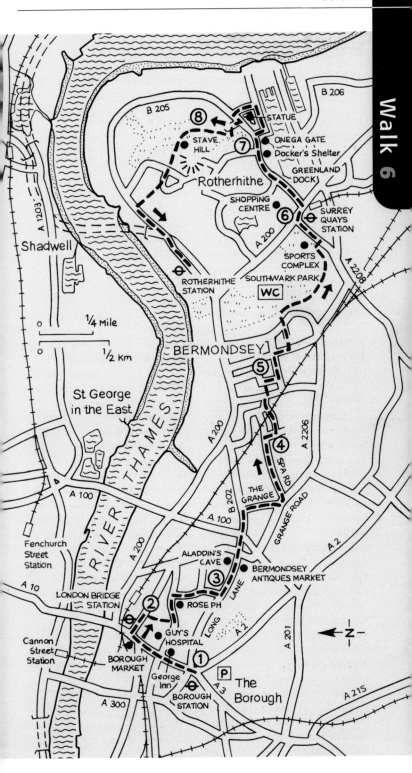

B 206

B 205

⑧

STAVE
HILL

Statue

⑦

ONEGA GATE

Docker's Shelter

GREENLAND
DOCK

Rotherhithe

SHOPPING
CENTRE

⑥

SURREY
QUAYS
STATION

A 200

A 2208

Shadwell

SPORTS
COMPLEX

SOUTHWARK PARK

ROTHERHITHE
STATION

WC

A 1203

BERMONDSEY

¼ Mile

½ Km

⑤

St George
in the East

A 200

A 2206

④

SPA RD

THE
GRANGE

GRANGE ROAD

B 202

A 100

A 2

A 100

RIVER THAMES

Fenchurch
Street
Station

ALADDIN'S
CAVE

BERMONDSEY
ANTIQUES MARKET

A 10

③

LONG LANE

A 2

A 200

LONDON BRIDGE
STATION

②

ROSE PH

A 201

N

Cannon
Street
Station

GUY'S
HOSPITAL

①

BOROUGH
MARKET

George Inn

P

The
Borough

A 300

A 3

BOROUGH
STATION

A 215

**Walk 6**

## Walk 6 Directions

① From **Borough tube** turn left to cross **Marshalsea Road** and continue along **Borough High Street**, ignoring the left-hand slip road. A few paces past London Bridge tube is **Borough Market**. Just after **Bedale Road** cross the road into **St Thomas Street**.

② Take the first right into **Great Maze Pond**, which runs between the buildings of Guy's Hospital. At the end turn left into **Snowsfields**. At the **Rose** pub turn right into **Weston Street** and continue past the original site of the Bermondsey Leather Market, to **Long Lane**.

> **WHERE TO EAT AND DRINK** ℹ
> The **George** in Borough High Street is London's last remaining galleried inn, where plays would be performed from the courtyard. It was a coaching inn in the 17th century and is now preserved by the National Trust.

③ Turn left and follow Long Lane until you reach some traffic lights. On the right is the **Bermondsey Antiques Market**. Carry on ahead, then turn right into The Grange. At the end turn left into **Grange Road**, then first left into **Spa Road**.

④ Just before the railway arch turn right into **Rouel Road** and then first left and under the railway arch. At the end turn right into **St James's Road**, cross the road and take the path on the left through some wooden posts.

⑤ Turn right, then take the second road on the left and, at the end, turn right. After 60yds (55m) turn left into **Southwark Park**, entering through the right-hand set of gates.

Turn right and follow as the path gently swings to the left; the exit is before the sports complex. Turn left along **Hawkestone Road** to **Surrey Quays tube station**.

> **WHILE YOU'RE THERE** ℹ
> Climb the 60 steps up to the top of **Stave Hill** for a panoramic view of London including the London Eye. The adjacent **Ecological Park** with its wind turbine is worth a visit too.

⑥ After crossing at the lights take the road behind the station leading into **Redriff Road**, which then veers left beside the shopping complex.

⑦ Just before the red **Onega Gate** turn right, signposted 'Russia Dock Woodland'. At the bottom of the steps turn left, past a row of town houses beside **Greenland Dock**. Turn left after the statue of James Walker and, ignoring the first path, turn left under a bridge and continue on the left-hand path (take the main path to the right if it is muddy).

⑧ Continue ahead, signposted 'Stave Hill', and turn next left. Walk in an anti-clockwise direction and follow the path opposite the steps to **Stave Hill** that leads to **Dock Hill Avenue**. This crosses two roads before reaching **Surrey Water**. With this to your left, head for the main road and once there, turn left and **Rotherhithe tube** is on the right.

> **WHAT TO LOOK FOR** ℹ
> Just before the Onega Gate in Redriff Road is a **dockers' shelter**. It was a hard life, for dockers were casual labourers who had to wait under this black awning each morning in the hope of being chosen for work. The number of men needed depended upon how many ships there were to unload.

# Old and New in Docklands

*Wandering through the Docklands, home to the world's oldest police force.*

| | |
|---|---|
| •DISTANCE• | 3½ miles (5.7km) |
| •MINIMUM TIME• | 1hr 45min |
| •ASCENT / GRADIENT• | Negligible ▲ ▲ ▲ |
| •LEVEL OF DIFFICULTY• | 𝕏 𝕏 𝕏 |
| •PATHS• | Paved streets and riverside paths |
| •LANDSCAPE• | Wharfs and docklands |
| •SUGGESTED MAP• | aqua3 OS Explorer 173 London North |
| •START• | Grid reference TQ 335807; Tower Hill tube |
| •FINISH• | Grid reference TQ 364803; Canary Wharf DLR |
| •DOG FRIENDLINESS• | On lead |
| •PUBLIC TOILETS• | None on route |

## BACKGROUND TO THE WALK

The Docklands has evolved from being one of the busiest ports in the world to being one of the most expensive dock developments. Yet there is a stillness to the area, as if the Victorian warehouses have not quite come to terms with their modern neighbours, of which the striking Canary Wharf complex is surely the best example.

While the police station in Wapping High Street is not open to the public, it is identified by the sign 'Metropolitan Police Marine Support', as the men and women here are responsible for policing the Thames. At the back of this listed building a pontoon, with its 'dead body tray' – where bodies are initially placed – sways gently on the river. Each year teams of river police and divers recover between 40 and 50 bodies and rescue more than 100 people from the river. Similar things happen on the water as on land: people get lost, things get stolen, and there are accidents and injuries. The only difference is that boats replace cars – and this watery highway is a tidal one.

In the 18th century many thousands of men worked in the docks handling imports that included fine cloth, precious metals and spices. Petty thefts were commonplace and there were around 100 pirates operating between London Bridge and Gravesend alone. Two men – John Harriott, a Justice of the Peace from Essex, and Patrick Colquhoun, a magistrate – decided to do something about it. In 1798 they obtained approval from Parliament to finance the first preventative policing of the river (the Metropolitan Police wasn't formed for another 30 years). It was a resounding success: within six months the Marine Police had saved an astounding £112,000 worth of cargo. But it wasn't until 1878, when the *Princess Alice* paddle steamer sank near Barking with the loss of over 600 lives, that the rowing galleys the Marine Police had been using were replaced with more powerful craft. Today the teams use Rigid Inflatable Boats (RIBs) and larger, more conventional vessels.

The compact museum in the police station contains some of the earliest exhibits of policing to be found. Although you must book all tours (minimum of six people), an officer will explain the interesting exhibits and show you the pontoon, and may even give their opinion of Captain Kidd. He was a fine sailor, who was hanged at nearby Execution Dock for piracy. Five years before, he had set sail for Boston but was later accused of robbing British ships and brought back to England for trial.

CANARY
WHARF DLR

Isle of Dogs

Poplar

Millwall

A 13

A 1261

A 1206

WESTFERRY
CIRCUS

⑥

PIER

⑦

Limehouse

RIVER THAMES

BARLEY
MOW PH

Ratcliff

½ Mile

½ Km

Rotherhithe

EDWARD VII
MEMORIAL PARK

B 205

PROSPECT OF
WHITBY PH

⑤

A 200

Shadwell

A 1203

A 13

POLICE STATION

④

IL BORDELLO

St George
in the East

Wapping

WAPPING HIGH ST

BERMONDSEY

A 200

③

GRAND
TURK

DICKENS
INN

Whitechapel

ST KATHERINE'S
DOCK

② Tower
Bridge

TOWER OF
LONDON

TOWER
HILL STA

①

Fenchurch St
Station

TRAITORS'
GATE

A 3

A 2206

REMAINS OF CITY WALL

**Walk 7 Walk 7 Directions**

① Take the underpass from **Tower Hill tube** that leads to the **Tower of London**. In front of the moat are the remains of the east gate of the medieval wall that once surrounded the City. Turn right and follow the path, taking the exit to the right of a ticket office. Turn left through the main gates to the Tower of London and follow the cobbled path for 440yds (402m).

---

**WHAT TO LOOK FOR** ⓘ

Rising to 800ft (244m), the **Canary Wharf Tower** is the flagship of the Canary Wharf development, so named because, when it was used as a dock, many of the imports were from the Canary Islands. The Tower has 50 floors and nearly 4,000 windows.

---

② Cross the road and enter **St Katherine's Dock**. Turn left, signposted 'Ivory House'. Bear right to cross a footbridge and pass some very stylish yachts and shops to cross the **Telford Footbridge**. Take the path between the *Grand Turk*, an 18th-century warship replica, and the **Dickens Inn** pub, then bear left through a private estate and right into **Mews Street**.

③ Turn right into **Thomas More Street** and, as the road swings to the right, it meets **Wapping High Street**. Turn left along this street of wharfs, luxury developments and Victorian warehouses. The blue-

---

**WHILE YOU'RE THERE** ⓘ

Each Sunday the **White Tower** in the Tower of London holds a service at 11AM so if you time it right and arrive 15 minutes in advance, you can take part. Go to the guard house in front of the Middle Tower to gain access.

---

and-white 1970s-style building on your right is the Metropolitan Police boat yard. Continue, to pass **Il Bordello** restaurant and the **police station**.

④ Continue ahead past Wapping tube and **Wapping Lane**. After the road bends to the left at **New Crane Wharf**, turn right into **Wapping Wall**, signposted 'Thames Path'. Just past the **Prospect of Whitby** pub cross a bridge over **Shadwell Basin**.

⑤ Turn right on to the riverside path and bear to the right of the **Edward VII Memorial Park** for a superb view of Canary Wharf. After a blue apartment block the path bends away from the river and joins **Narrow Street**; it later passes the **Barley Mow** pub as you cross the **Limehouse Basin**.

⑥ Turn right into **Three Colts Street** and walk to the end, where you meet the river again at the Canary Riverside path. Continue ahead to **Canary Wharf Pier**.

---

**WHERE TO EAT AND DRINK** ⓘ

You'll smell the garlic from **Il Bordello**, an Italian restaurant in Wapping High Street, long before you see it. The traditional food here is excellent. If you prefer pubs, you're really spoilt for choice. The **Dickens Inn**, St Katherine's Dock, has stripped bare boards and the **Prospect of Whitby** is one of the oldest riverside pubs in London.

---

⑦ Walk up the steps on the left of the pier, cross the road to **Westferry Circus** and continue in the direction of **Canary Wharf**, which is immediately ahead. Bear right to follow signs to Canary Wharf DLR, cutting through **Cabot Square** into **Cabot Place**, before arriving at the station entrance.

**Walk 8**

# Spending Measured Time Around Greenwich

*Discover more about the background to Greenwich Mean Time on a walk through Greenwich Park.*

| | |
|---|---|
| •DISTANCE• | 3½ miles (5.7km) |
| •MINIMUM TIME• | 1hr 45min |
| •ASCENT / GRADIENT• | 154ft (47m) ▲ ▲ ▲ |
| •LEVEL OF DIFFICULTY• | 🚶🚶 🚶🚶 🚶 |
| •PATHS• | Tarmac paths |
| •LANDSCAPE• | Parkland and superb views across London |
| •SUGGESTED MAP• | aqua3 OS Explorer 161 London South |
| •START / FINISH• | Grid reference TQ 382783; Island Gardens DLR |
| •DOG FRIENDLINESS• | On lead in foot tunnel |
| •PUBLIC TOILETS• | Greenwich Park and Pier |

## BACKGROUND TO THE WALK

Marcus Aurelius Antoninus once said 'Time is like a river made up of the events which happen… no sooner does anything appear than it is swept away, and another comes in its place'. Many centuries later, these words could have applied to the problems encountered at sea by captains and their crews where, over and over again, ships were wrecked because of a lack of navigational aids. Until the 17th century, captains could tell the ship's position of latitude by the stars and the sun, but longitude was a real problem: they had no way of telling how far east or west a ship was positioned.

### A Formidable Task

It was Charles II who rescued Greenwich after it fell on hard times under Oliver Cromwell. Previously the birthplace of Henry VIII and his daughters Mary I and Elizabeth I, Greenwich was given a Royal Observatory in 1675 to try to provide seafarers with more accurate charts. The first Astronomer Royal was John Flamsteed who took the job at the age of 28. During his 45 years at the observatory, he made more than 50,000 observations. There was just one problem – in this time he had not arrived at a solution for longitude. The last straw for the government came in 1707 when four Royal Navy ships sunk off the Isles of Scilly, claiming 2,000 lives. Parliament offered a reward of £20,000 for anyone finding a solution to the longitude problem. It was eventually claimed – by a clockmaker.

John Harrison (1693–1776) came down to London in 1730 with the idea that longitude could be worked out by using the time. His solution was based on the fact that for every 15 degrees travelled eastwards, the local time moves one hour ahead. Therefore, if we know the local times at two points on Earth, we can use the difference between them to calculate how far apart those places are in longitude, east or west. This idea was crucial to sailors in the 17th century. The problem was that every minute gained or lost could consequently amount to a navigational error of 15 nautical miles (17¼ miles or 28.9km) so the solution hinged on producing a clock that kept the exact time in turbulent conditions. Harrison made four clocks for this purpose. The first was designed to run consistently, regardless of movement or temperature changes. He made a second clock, then took 19 years to work on the third prototype, the H3. However, it was his fourth, the H4, which clinched the deal. The most compact, it was the forerunner of all precision watches and provided the basis for an accurate sea chronometer which finally enabled sailors to work out their exact position. Ironically, Harrison was well in to his seventies before he received any prize money. Despite the success of his machines, the committee responsible for paying him stalled repeatedly and only the intervention of King George III secured him recognition and his just reward.

In 1884 it was decided, at an international conference in Washington DC, that Greenwich should become the site of the prime meridian, an imaginary line running north to south, denoting the world's longitudinal zero. This means that every position on Earth is defined by its longitude (distance east or west) from Greenwich. With a little help from Charles II and Flamsteed, John Harrison left the world a timeless legacy.

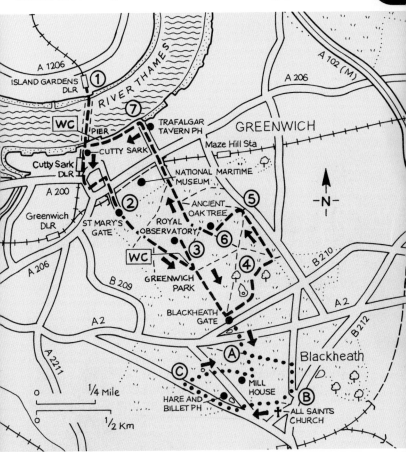

## Walk 8 Directions

① From **Island Gardens DLR** cross the Thames by the foot tunnel. With the *Cutty Sark* on your left,

cross the road ahead into **Greenwich Church Street**. After a further 70yds (64m) turn left into the market. At the far end turn right and follow **King William Walk** to **Greenwich Park**.

**Walk 8**

② Enter the park at **St Mary's Gate** and follow the wide path, known as **The Avenue**, as it swings to the left. Continue ahead, turning left at the toilets to reach the **Royal Observatory** and a superb view over London and the Greenwich Royal Naval College.

③ Retrace your steps, past the Royal Observatory's Planetarium building and a café to follow this broad pathway, **Blackheath Avenue**. Just before **Blackheath Gate** turn left through some metal gates along a path that skirts the edge of a large pond. (A tiny path a few paces further on the right leads into an area for viewing the deer.)

> **WHILE YOU'RE THERE** ⓘ
>
> Spare a thought for the peasants who, led by Wat Tyler, gathered on **Blackheath** in revolt against their feudal serfdom in 1381. As labourers were scarce after the ravages of the Black Death, they were in a good position to demand better pay, but a bill was passed to ensure they could earn no more than a decreed amount. The Peasants Revolt saw popular uprisings throughout southern England. The Lord Chancellor and Archbishop of Canterbury were murdered, before Tyler was betrayed and killed near Smithfield in the City.

④ Turn right at the next fork and exit gates to the enclosure. Turn left and take the right-hand fork. Continue along this straight path beside a wall.

> **WHAT TO LOOK FOR** ⓘ
>
> The **Greenwich Foot Tunnel** was built in 1902 to link Greenwich with the Isle of Dogs, so workers from south London could get to the docks. The wood-panelled lifts that take you underground were replaced in the 1990s. They are enormous and quite a contrast from the starkness of the foot tunnel. The lift attendants also have use of a small electric heater in winter so, if you're not warm after the 400yd (366m) walk along the foot tunnel, you soon will be.

⑤ At the next junction take the second path on the left and keep ahead, straight over another set of paths, to reach another junction at which an oak tree is protected by railings. This dates from the 12th century and lived to a ripe old age of 700 years. It is said that Anne Boleyn danced around the tree with Henry VIII and their daughter, Elizabeth, would often play in the hollow trunk of the huge oak.

⑥ Turn right, downhill, and right again at the next junction on a path that dips and rises. Continue ahead at the next set of paths and leave the park at **Park Row Gate**. Keep ahead along **Park Row**, past the National Maritime Museum and across **Romney Road**.

⑦ At the **Trafalgar Tavern** turn left along the **Thames Path** to reach **Greenwich Pier**. Retrace your steps along the **Greenwich Foot Tunnel** to **Island Gardens DLR**.

> **WHERE TO EAT AND DRINK**
>
> The **Trafalgar Tavern** is a large riverside pub with a grand, wood-panelled dining room that was famous for its 'white-bait suppers' in the 19th century. Dickens mentions this room in his novel, *Our Mutual Friend*. Nowadays, the menu still features fish along with traditional English dishes such as sausages and mash, and lamb with rosemary. On Walk 9 you will pass the **Hare and Billet** pub, which has a privileged position by the heath. It offers a Sunday roast and a good variety of Belgian beer including Bellevue, Duvel and Hoegaarden.

# Overtime in Green Blackheath

*Allow a little more time for this short extension to the expanse of grass that forms Blackheath.*
See map and information panel for Walk 8

| | |
|---|---|
| **•DISTANCE•** | ¾ mile (1.2km) |
| **•MINIMUM TIME•** | 30min |
| **•ASCENT / GRADIENT•** | Negligible |
| **•LEVEL OF DIFFICULTY•** | |

## Walk 9 Directions (Walk 8 option)

Follow Walk 8 but instead of turning left before **Blackheath Gate**, go through it, cross the road on the other side and follow the road towards the A2, here **Shooter's Hill Road**, Point Ⓐ.

Everything here is orderly and spacious. On a fine day the local prep schools make full use of the heath. Stopping to check my map, four girls, eager to help, rushed over to ask if I was lost. They told me that it's called Blackheath after the Black Death ' …because the bodies are buried under our feet'. As feasible as this might seem, it's not strictly true, because the name was already established 200 years before the plague wiped out one quarter of the European population around 1348. More prosaically, the name probably derives from the colour of the dark soil here when it gets wet. (Sorry, girls.)

Walk along **Duke Humphrey Road** towards the spire of All Saints Church. At a crossroad of paths

ahead turn left and then right into **Prince Charles Road**. Just before the road swerves, turn right along a narrow path towards the church, Point Ⓑ. Keeping to the right of the church, turn right along a path to reach a mini-roundabout. Cross diagonally into **Hare and Billet Road**, then go past a pond and the pub. Some 50yds (46m) after the heath on the left meets the road, cross the road and take the path on your right (Point Ⓒ).

Following the Peasants' Revolt in 1381, rebels also camped here in 1450, during John Cade's rebellion against Henry VI's government. In 1497 a large army of Cornishmen marched here to protest against tax increases and the war in Scotland. After widespread desertions, the remainder of the West Country force was crushed by troops loyal to Henry VII and their leaders were executed.

After another pond continue ahead at the road junction, along **Talbot Place**. At the T-junction, shortly after the white building of **Mill House**, turn left and retrace your steps back to **Blackheath Gate**, where you can rejoin Walk 8.

# Finsbury Park's Buffer Zone

*Following a disused railway on a green route to Alexandra Palace.*

| | |
|---|---|
| •DISTANCE• | 4½ miles (7.2km) |
| •MINIMUM TIME• | 2hrs |
| •ASCENT / GRADIENT• | 197ft (60m) ▲▲▲ |
| •LEVEL OF DIFFICULTY• | 🚶 🚶 🚶 |
| •PATHS• | Mainly gravel paths |
| •LANDSCAPE• | Green corridor through built-up areas of north London |
| •SUGGESTED MAP• | aqua3 OS Explorer 173 London North |
| •START / FINISH• | Grid reference TQ 313868; Finsbury Park tube and bus |
| •DOG FRIENDLINESS• | No particular problems |
| •PUBLIC TOILETS• | None on route |

## Walk 10 Directions

This is a linear walk with the option of taking a short bus ride back to the start. You don't have to be a train-spotter to appreciate it and indeed, it might help if you're not – trains no longer run here.

Enter the **Parkland Walk** from **Stroud Green Road** through an entrance in the wall. Follow the curving path that initially runs alongside a railway line and then, to the right, overlooks Finsbury Park. At a T-junction turn left and cross a footbridge over the railway. Turn sharp right to continue along the disused railway track that once connected Finsbury Park with Alexandra Palace.

The trackbed has been converted into a parkland walk that alternates between running along the top of an embankment and through the deep, wooded cuttings of the original railway. It is London's longest statutory Local Nature Reserve and, although King's Cross at one point is a mere 3 miles

(4.8km) further south, you'll feel totally detached from the bustle of urban life.

Continue for a further 1½ miles (2.4km) along this attractive pathway with nine bridges, which at one point passes between former station platforms.

In its heyday in the 1870s, the Finsbury Park-to-Alexandra Palace line carried 60,000 passengers on one Whit Monday. Its demise was due to the advent of electric trains and the opening of the Hampstead to Highgate tube. Ironically, in

---

**WHILE YOU'RE THERE**

Haringey's conservation staff can be justly proud of their 2 acre (0.8ha) **Railway Fields Nature Reserve**, near Manor House tube. It's the only one of its kind in Haringey. This used to be a railway goods yard and, although coal can still be found, the only trace of its past life is a set of old rails and a couple of buffers. There's a pond, woodland scrub and a meadow. The unique 'Haringey Knotweed' was discovered here in 1987. It's a cross between the Russian vine and a Japanese knotweed.

Walk 10

are now heading away from the road and following the Capital Ring path. It swings to the right and descends gradually through this woodland that is so dense and ancient that Hansel and Gretel wouldn't look out of place here. Notice the grand oak tree clad with fungi and shaped like a totem pole.

At a T-junction turn left, past the former wood-keeper's cottage to **Muswell Hill Road**. Cross this at the traffic lights and enter **Highgate Wood**. Take the path on the right-hand side and continue through the woods until the path runs parallel with a row of houses. Turn right here, to leave the wood at the northern end of Muswell Hill Road. Cross the road, turn right into **Cranleigh Gardens** and, almost immediately, take the path on the left of a garden centre. At the bottom of the steps turn right to rejoin the railway path. Here you can enjoy views to the mast of Alexandra Park and as far as Canary Wharf, in Docklands.

1954, when the last train ran, it had to be lengthened from two to eight carriages to meet public demand.

Eventually, you veer left up a path, lined with wooden posts, that leads to a road. Turn right out of the gate, right at the **Shepherds** pub and right again, into **Shepherds Hill**. Here you will see a library on the opposite side of the road. Turn left immediately in front of it and follow the rough track that descends to **Priory Gardens**.

Turn right and, after about 250yds (229m), turn left along an alleyway between houses, which leads to the 50 acre (20ha) **Queens Wood**. The path climbs gently to cross **Queens Wood Road** and continues bearing left through Queens Wood. After 50yds (46m) turn sharp left. At a crossroads of paths turn right. You

Go through an underpass and a covered walkway to bear right along a path through **Alexandra Park** that passes a café. Continue through the gates, and cross the road on the right to catch the W3 bus back to **Finsbury Park bus station** (a 15 minute journey).

# Guts and Garters in the Ripper's East End

*Tracing the path of the world's most notorious serial killer, Jack the Ripper, in London's East End.*

| | |
|---|---|
| •DISTANCE• | 2¾ miles (4.4km) |
| •MINIMUM TIME• | 1hr 30min |
| •ASCENT / GRADIENT• | Negligible |
| •LEVEL OF DIFFICULTY• | |
| •PATHS• | Paved streets |
| •LANDSCAPE• | Plenty of narrow streets and some main roads |
| •SUGGESTED MAP• | AA Street by Street London |
| •START / FINISH• | Aldgate tube |
| •DOG FRIENDLINESS• | On lead |
| •PUBLIC TOILETS• | None on route |

## BACKGROUND TO THE WALK

Although the thick 'pea souper' fogs no longer exist, the East End can still be pretty grim. However, just when you're adapting to the greyness, you'll notice another fascinating alley and building to explore. A few years after the Jack the Ripper murders some of the original street names were changed to avoid notoriety; other sites are now buried beneath new buildings, but this walk will take you very close to all five sites. But be quick – the developers are moving faster than you can say Jack the Ripper.

### The World's Most Notorious Serial Killer

In the space of 10 weeks during the autumn of 1888 five women, all prostitutes, were brutally murdered. At the time, Whitechapel was home to the poor and destitute and pollution from sewers was commonplace. If you didn't die of hunger then you had a high chance of succumbing to disease. Infant mortality was soaring. Over 80 per cent of the population were considered criminals. Given these facts, prostitution may not have seemed such a bad option for many women. As illiteracy was high among the poor, no doubt news of the killings was spread by word of mouth, although in the literate world at the time, the murder of a prostitute would hardly have raised too many eyebrows. More than 100 years later the murderer's true identity remains a mystery. Jack the Ripper has become one of the most notorious serial killers of all time and the subject of many films and documentaries.

### Modus Operandi

The first victim, 42-year-old Mary Ann Nichols, was found with her throat cut from left to right, suggesting that the killer was left-handed; her stomach had also been slashed several times. Annie Chapman, aged 47, was the second victim and, as well as having her throat cut, certain organs had been skilfully removed from her abdomen. The third victim, 45-year-old Elizabeth Stride, also had her throat cut, but apparently a passing pony and trap, driven by the man who discovered her corpse, interrupted the killer. Victim number four was Catherine Eddowes, aged 46, who was found less than an hour after Stride. Her uterus and left kidney had been removed – the kidney was later sent to the chairman of the Whitechapel Vigilance Committee in a package along with a note.

Crowds began to gather at the murder sites and vigilante groups became increasingly active, frustrated by the apparent failings of the police investigation. Records show that the Ripper was able to spend more time with his last victim, Mary Jane Kelly. She was the only one in her twenties, and was murdered at her home. However, she was so badly mutilated she could be identified only by her eyes and hair.

## Walk 11 Directions

① With **Aldgate tube station** behind you, walk towards **St Botolph's Church** on the right. Cross the road at the pedestrian lights and continue ahead, past the school on the corner. Turn right along **Mitre Street**. A few paces further is **Mitre Square**, where the

fourth body, Catherine Eddowes, was discovered by the benches.

② Continue ahead, turning right into **Creechurch Lane** and past some posts marking the boundaries of the City of London. Go across two main roads to reach **Stoney Lane**. Bear right into **Gravel Lane** and, at the end, past the parade of shops, turn left along **Middlesex**

**Walk 11**

**Street**. Take the first right into **Wentworth Street**, more commonly called Petticoat Lane and host to the famous, thriving market.

③ Turn left into **Bell Lane** and right into **Brune Street**, where you'll see the remains of a Victorian soup kitchen. At the end turn left and left again into **White's Row**, where the fifth body, that of Mary Jane Kelly, was found (the site is now a car park). Cross **Bell Lane** and follow **Artillery Lane** as it narrows to form an alleyway.

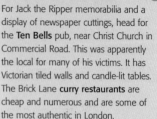

> **WHILE YOU'RE THERE** ⓘ
> The markets here are the best in London. Petticoat Lane and its subsidiaries form a river of market stalls, especially on a Sunday morning, when you'll be able to pick a bargain or two. Spitalfields Market is under cover and tends to consist mainly of crafts and fashion stalls.

④ Turn right into **Sandy's Row**, past a synagogue, then right and left to reach **Brushfield Street**. This passes **Spitalfields Market** and ends up at Hawksmoor's majestic Christ Church Spitalfields, the white building ahead. Cross **Commercial Street** at the pedestrian lights and turn left.

⑤ As the road bends turn right into **Hanbury Street**, where the Truman's Brewery denotes the murder scene of the second victim,

> **WHAT TO LOOK FOR** ⓘ
> Between 1880 and 1914 Whitechapel became home to hundreds of eastern European, Jewish refugees. The soup kitchen in Brune Street is evidence of this. Here, the 'Jewish Poor' as they were called, came for some basic hot soup. Notice the Dickensian 'Way In' and 'Way Out' signs above the doors.

> **WHERE TO EAT AND DRINK** ⓘ
> For Jack the Ripper memorabilia and a display of newspaper cuttings, head for the **Ten Bells** pub, near Christ Church in Commercial Road. This was apparently the local for many of his victims. It has Victorian tiled walls and candle-lit tables. The Brick Lane curry restaurants are cheap and numerous and are some of the most authentic in London.

Annie Chapman. Cross **Brick Lane** and continue along this road for another 500yds (457m), past the Brady Recreation Centre and along an alleyway.

⑥ Turn right into the main road and cross over at the pedestrian lights. On the left Durward Street leads to the site of the first murder, where Mary Ann Nichols' body was found, but little now remains of the original streets. Instead continue ahead and cross the busy stream of traffic on **Whitechapel Road** into **New Road**.

⑦ When you get to **Fieldgate Street** turn right towards the austere buildings of a former synagogue and then take the third left into **Settles Street**. When you reach the end bear right and cross over at the pedestrian lights, to turn left into **Henriques Street**. The school here stands on the site of the Ripper's third victim, Elizabeth Stride.

⑧ Continue ahead, following the road at it swings to the right. At the end, turn left and then immediately right into **Hooper Street** and right again into **Leman Street**. Cross the road into **Alie Street**. At the end bear right and then left along **Little Somerset Street**, which comes out opposite where you began the walk at **Aldgate tube**.

# Corridors of Power

*A look at some of the city's landmarks, from Whitehall through to Smithfield.*

| | |
|---|---|
| **•DISTANCE•** | 4 miles (6.4km) |
| **•MINIMUM TIME•** | 2hrs 30min |
| **•ASCENT / GRADIENT•** | Negligible |
| **•LEVEL OF DIFFICULTY•** | |
| **•PATHS•** | Paved streets |
| **•LANDSCAPE•** | Main processional routes, busy streets |
| **•SUGGESTED MAP•** | AA Street by Street London |
| **•START•** | Westminster tube |
| **•FINISH•** | Farringdon tube |
| **•DOG FRIENDLINESS•** | A dog's nightmare |
| **•PUBLIC TOILETS•** | Westminster, Strand |

## BACKGROUND TO THE WALK

It's easy to take sights for granted in a city where, around every bend, is another symbol of its historic importance. Hopefully, this walk, through some of the better-known parts, will sharpen your senses and alert you to some of the buildings and streets you may be familiar with, and others that you have yet to notice. It's best to avoid this walk on Mondays when some of the places mentioned are closed.

The walk begins across the road from the Houses of Parliament at Westminster Abbey, where every king and queen since 1066 has been crowned and where many are buried. On a corner opposite Horse Guards Parade is one of the best places to stand for a grandstand view of the Queen's carriage as it heads up Whitehall for the State Opening of Parliament. We move on to the Strand, once one of the most influential thoroughfares in Britain with many fine mansions, some of which you can still see today. One of these is the magnificent Somerset House, which has awesome grounds for central London and is much-loved by film companies for its grandeur and seclusion.

The street names from here on give a clue to the past inhabitants. Think of dukes and earls – Arundel, Surrey and Essex – as the Strand enters Aldwych (a name that derives from 'Old Wic' meaning old settlement). The grand buildings in this area are symbols of the architectural legacy of the Empire. If you're after proof, notice how Canada House, the South African Embassy and the Australian High Commission each take pride of place in Trafalgar Square, the Strand and Aldwych respectively. Where the Strand ends and Fleet Street begins are a number of banks. These serviced those working at the Inns of Court, including Lloyds Bank with its floral tiles, and Child & Co Bankers. The latter has a display of guns in a cabinet that the partners of the bank acquired during the Gordon Riots of 1780 'for the defence of the building'. Here too is one of the first cheques – made out in 1705.

We end the walk by another church, St Bartholomew-the-Great, which dates from 1123 and is still surrounded by small streets as it was in the Middle Ages. Near by is Smithfield, the scene of jousting, tournaments and fairs and the site for executions where criminals were not just hanged but boiled, roasted or burnt. During the Peasant's Revolt of 1381 the rebel leader Wat Tyler was stabbed by the Lord Mayor William Walworth and taken to St Bartholomew's Hospital but soldiers dragged him out and decapitated him.

Walk 12

## Walk 12 Directions

① Leave **Westminster tube** following signs to the Houses of Parliament. Cross **Abingdon Street** to **Westminster Abbey** and the adjacent St Margaret's Church. Turn back along Abingdon Street and continue ahead as the road becomes **Parliament Street**, and then **Whitehall**. Follow it past the Cenotaph, a simple block of

Portland Stone that commemorates those people who died in the First and Second World Wars, all the way to **Trafalgar Square**.

② Turn right here and cross **Northumberland Avenue**. Turn right into the **Strand**, the road that links Westminster with the City of London. Turn right at **Savoy Street**, to see the Queen's Chapel of the Savoy; otherwise carry on along the Strand, past **Somerset House**.

**Walk 12**

③ Turn right into **Surrey Street**, past the Roman Baths, left into **Temple Place** and left again along **Arundel Street**. The two churches in the middle of the road are St Mary-le-Strand and St Clement Danes. After these the road becomes **Fleet Street**.

④ After the banks of Lloyds and Child & Co turn right into **Whitefriars Street**. At the end turn left and left again into **Dorset Rise**. Take the next right into Dorset Buildings, past the Bridewell Theatre and along **Bride Lane** to St Bride's Church. Cross **New Bridge Street**.

⑤ You are now in Ludgate Hill. Turn left into the street called **Old Bailey** and continue to the Central Criminal Court, known as 'The Old Bailey' – it lies on the site of the notorious former Newgate Prison.

Cross **Newgate Street** and follow **Giltspur Street** to reach St Bartholomew's Hospital.

⑥ Walk under the archway to the hospital, with the only remaining sculpture of Henry VIII, to visit St Bartholomew-the-Less, the parish church of the hospital where the Stuart architect Inigo Jones was baptised. As you continue past the central square opposite Smithfield Market, notice the marks on the stone wall left by a Zeppelin raid during the First World War. At St Bartholomew-the-Great turn left into **Hayne Street** and again into **Charterhouse Street**.

### *WHAT TO LOOK FOR*

**St John's Gate** was the main entrance to the Grand Priory in Clerkenwell and later a coffee house run by Richard Hogarth, father of the painter William. When the nave of the church was blown up the stone was used by the Lord Protectorate in 1550, to rebuild his palace on the Strand, known as Somerset House.

⑦ At **St John Street** turn right and then bear left into **St John's Lane**. A few paces further on you will find **St John's Gate**. Keep going to reach Grand Priory Church, bear left to **Jerusalem Passage**, then turn left at the end, on to **Aylesbury Street**. Cross **Clerkenwell Street** and walk along **Britton Street**, turning right into **Benjamin Street** to reach **Farringdon tube** where the walk ends.

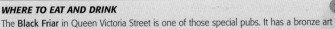

### *WHERE TO EAT AND DRINK*

The **Black Friar** in Queen Victoria Street is one of those special pubs. It has a bronze art nouveau/Edwardian interior and tongue-in-cheek phrases such as 'haste is slow' and 'wisdom is rare' written above the doorways. The back room will leave you gaping in wonderment. There are bar snacks, ales on hand-pump and gallons of atmosphere. If the **Jerusalem Tavern** in Britton Street reminds you of an old style coffee house, don't be surprised because that is what it once was. Now it's cavernous and hugely attractive and serves an interesting selection of beers, including organic wheat beer.

**Walk 13**

# The Bright Side of Balham

*A circular route highlighting the greener spots of Balham and its most famous art deco property.*

| | |
|---|---|
| **·DISTANCE·** | 3 miles (4.8km) |
| **·MINIMUM TIME·** | 1hr 30min |
| **·ASCENT / GRADIENT·** | 33ft (10m) ▲▲▲ |
| **·LEVEL OF DIFFICULTY·** | 🏃 🏃 🏃 |
| **·PATHS·** | Paved streets, tarmac and gravel paths across commons |
| **·LANDSCAPE·** | Urban greenery |
| **·SUGGESTED MAP·** | aqua3 OS Explorer 161 London South |
| **·START / FINISH·** | Grid reference TQ 285731 Balham Station (tube and rail) |
| **·DOG FRIENDLINESS·** | No particular problems |
| **·PUBLIC TOILETS·** | None on route |

## BACKGROUND TO THE WALK

When I tell people that I live in Balham, it never fails to amaze me how many knowingly answer with that old chestnut: 'Ah, you mean the Gateway to the South'. The catch-phrase, made famous by Peter Sellers, seems set to stay around for a few more decades. Fortunately, Balham has much more to offer than mere access to south London – some might even say it has had the last laugh.

### Huguenots and Hitler

Balham is mentioned in the Domesday Book. In the late 18th century it mainly consisted of fields peppered with large houses. In the 1860s, by the time the railway network had increased, it was already popular with the working and middle classes and residential developments began to appear. In the 1930s the architect G Kay Green designed the largest privately-owned block under one roof in Europe. Du Cane Court, named after a family of Huguenots on whose land the site was built, contains 676 flats and is home to more than 1,000 residents. When the Second World War began many people left for the relative safety of the countryside but the Foreign Office came to the rescue: many of its staff rented a flat in the block, no doubt impressed by the short train journey to Victoria. In the 1940s a small flat cost around £6 a month to rent, which was not considered cheap but it included a remarkable view. Today, from the seventh floor rooftop, the panoramic view over London must surely match those from Parliament Hill, Alexandra Palace, Canary Wharf and anywhere else north of the river, for that matter.

Despite being a major landmark in the area, because of its size, it was never bombed by the Germans during the war (although 64 lives were lost when Balham Station was hit). Some even say that Hitler had placed spies here and that it was used as a landmark by his aircrews. If this were true, the spies would have been in good hands for, food rations permitting, the restaurant on the top floor served some very fine dishes.

### Comic Balhamites

Margaret Rutherford, the comedy actress who became a household name after starring as Miss Marple was born here in 1892. Also born here, but in 1946, was John Sullivan, who

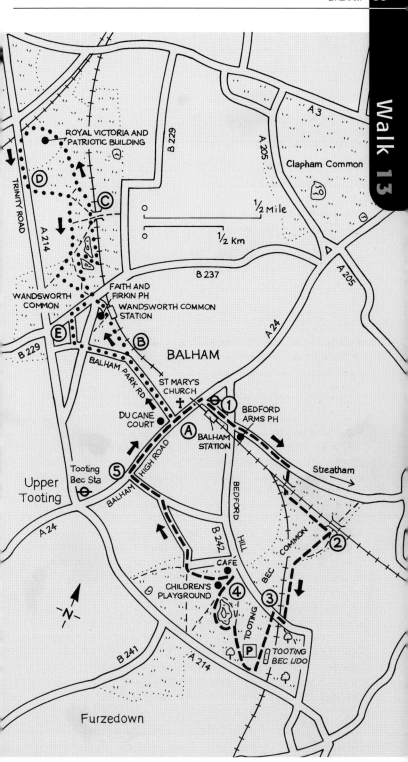

ROYAL VICTORIA AND
PATRIOTIC BUILDING

Ⓓ

TRINITY ROAD

A 214

Ⓒ

B 229

A 205

A 3

Clapham Common

½ Mile

½ Km

B 237

A 205

A 24

WANDSWORTH
COMMON

FAITH AND
FIRKIN PH

WANDSWORTH COMMON
STATION

Ⓔ

B 229

Ⓑ

BALHAM

BALHAM PARK RD

ST MARY'S
CHURCH

DU CANE
COURT

Ⓐ

Ⓞ①

BEDFORD
ARMS PH

BALHAM
STATION

Streatham

Upper
Tooting

Tooting
Bec Sta

⑤

BALHAM

HIGH ROAD

BEDFORD HILL

BEC COMMON

②

A 24

B 242

CAFE

CHILDREN'S
PLAYGROUND

④

③

TOOTING

Ⓟ

TOOTING
BEC LIDO

B 241

A 214

Furzedown

N

Walk 13

wrote *Citizen Smith* and the timeless *Only Fools and Horses* for television. If you want to see the interior of Du Cane Court, you'll have to watch one of the Agatha Christie adaptations in which the lobby and flats have been featured; the sweeping art deco staircase is indeed a rare and wonderful sight.

## Walk 13 Directions

① Turn right at **Balham station**, along **Balham Station Road**. Cross at the lights, past the **Bedford Arms** pub, into **Fernlea Road**. At a mini-roundabout turn right before a strip of common and go under a railway bridge. Turn left and follow the wall of the railway embankment, passing a playground and playing fields on the right.

---

**WHAT TO LOOK FOR** ⓘ

Hamilton House, on the right of Balham High Road is the Polish White Eagle Club used by many of Balham's Polish immigrants who settled here after the Second World War. On the opposite side of the road is the red brick Polish Catholic church, Christ the King.

---

② At another bridge take the right-hand tarmac path running parallel to a row of houses. As the path bends to the left, it runs alongside another railway track lined with trees before meeting a road, **Bedford Hill**. Turn right and cross the road to join a path across **Tooting Bec Common**.

③ Turn sharp left and continue along a path that hugs the railway track and passes **Tooting Bec Lido**. Pass the Lido car park and follow the path that circles it clockwise. After crossing the car park approach road, take the right-hand path leading into the common and, at a clump of trees, turn left along a narrow path around a lake.

④ Beyond the children's playground take the next left to the café and follow this path until you reach **Hillbury Road**. Turn right at the crossroads and continue ahead into **Manville Road**. At the next crossroads turn left into **Ritherdon Road** and continue to the end.

⑤ Turn right at the traffic lights into **Balham High Road**, passing Du Cane Court and **St Mary's Church** before reaching the station from where the walk began.

---

**WHILE YOU'RE THERE** ⓘ

During the summer months, if your lungs are strong, take your swimming gear on the walk and visit the gigantic **Tooting Bec Lido** where even one width of the pool is a breathtaking 108ft (33m). Lidos are larger than life and this one, with its endearing wooden cubicle doors painted in bright, Caribbean shades, is no exception. On a hot summer's day it can get as many as 6,000 visitors.

---

**WHERE TO EAT AND DRINK** ⓘ

The **Bedford Arms** is a comfortable, airy sort of pub with sofas and a fireplace. At weekends it's like a chameleon, turning into one of London's premier comedy clubs favoured by both comics and punters. The quirky theatre is balconied with an ornate, domed ceiling and tables in the intimate 'overflow' room are decorated with candles. When the laughter ends it turns into a nightclub until 2AM. The **café** on Tooting Bec Common serves all-day breakfasts, burgers, and sausage and chips. It claims to be open seven days a week except at Christmas.

**Walk 14**

# And West to Wandsworth

*Discover the peculiarities of Balham's manicured common, flanked by an old asylum and a prison.*
See map and information panel for Walk 13

| | |
|---|---|
| •DISTANCE• | 3¼ miles (5.3km) |
| •MINIMUM TIME• | 1¾hrs |
| •ASCENT / GRADIENT• | 49ft (15m) ▲ ▲ ▲ |
| •LEVEL OF DIFFICULTY• | 🚶 🚶 🚶 |

## Walk 14 Directions
(Walk 13 option)

Leave Walk 13 at Point Ⓐ and turn left into **Balham Park Road**. Continue until the road swerves to the left and at this point, turn right into an alley between houses, signposted to Wandsworth Common railway station, Point Ⓑ.

Follow this tarmac path, the **Capital Ring**, along the edge of the common, past the station and its car park. At the traffic lights adjacent to the **Faith and Firkin** pub, cross the roads to reach three paths branching across the common. Take the middle path and follow it for 150yds (137m) and then take a path on the right towards a pond, following this round to the left. Cross a stone bridge, bear left and continue along a footpath running beside the railway line. Pass a bridge to your right, Point Ⓒ.

Just past the bowling green, follow the path leading off to the left across the field. Go through a gate into **Muir Drive**. Follow the path, which runs alongside the **Royal Victoria and Patriotic Building**

and before a bridge turn left to join a path with a set of 30 steps.

The rather grand and Gothic Royal Victoria and Patriotic Building now houses luxury apartments, workshops and a drama school. Its original function, when it opened in 1857, was as an asylum for orphans of the Crimean War.

Turn left along **Trinity Road**. To the south west and parallel to Trinity Road is Wandsworth Prison where Oscar Wilde spent six months in 1895. Follow **Trinity Road** for 350yds (320m), then turn left again, along a tarmac path to rejoin the common, Point Ⓓ. After two upright wooden posts, turn sharp right along the **Wandsworth Common Trim Trail**. Follow this wide track until you reach a crossing of paths. Turn right, then take the next left-hand fork along a path that is lined with sycamore trees. At the end turn left. Turn right at the next crossroads and continue back to **Bellevue Road**. Cross this, heading right, and turn left into **Althorp Road**, Point Ⓔ. Now turn left into **Nottingham Road**. Cross **St James's Road** to join **Balham Park Road**, retracing your footsteps from Point Ⓑ to Point Ⓐ and rejoining Walk 13.

Walk 15

# Find Yourself Doing the Lambeth Walk

*An easy stroll through Charlie Chaplin's home town, an aromatic garden and the Archbishop's Park.*

| | |
|---|---|
| •DISTANCE• | 3 miles (4.8km) |
| •MINIMUM TIME• | 1hr 30min |
| •ASCENT / GRADIENT• | Negligible |
| •LEVEL OF DIFFICULTY• | |
| •PATHS• | Mainly paved streets |
| •LANDSCAPE• | Riverside walk and churchyard garden |
| •SUGGESTED MAP• | aqua3 OS Explorer 161 London South |
| •START / FINISH• | Grid reference TQ304780; Vauxhall tube |
| •DOG FRIENDLINESS• | Keep on lead |
| •PUBLIC TOILETS• | Archbishop's Park |

## Walk 15 Directions

This is the closest you will get to Lambeth Palace, which, although not open to the public, can be seen from the adjoining Archbishop's Park, a recreation ground still owned by the Archbishop of Canterbury. It is also the area in which Charlie Chaplin grew up and the one that started the dance craze in the 1930s, the Lambeth Walk, used in the musical *Me and My Girl* (1937). And last but not least, this walk includes a church that has been turned into a quirky museum dedicated to the history of gardening.

Take Exit 6 from **Vauxhall tube**, turn left and walk over a pedestrian footbridge, towards the green-tinted windows of the **MI6 building**. After 100yds (91m) turn left along a path towards the river to join the **Thames Path** and follow this along to the right. At **Lambeth Bridge** follow the underpass to the right of

the steps leading up to the bridge and, once through to the other side, you'll catch a glimpse of the Houses of Parliament on the opposite bank. A few steps further on, turn right, opposite the steps to Thames Cruises, and cross the road to **St Mary-at-Lambeth Church**. To your left is the entrance to the Archbishop of Canterbury's London pad, **Lambeth Palace**.

Continue through the churchyard and enter the **Museum of Garden History**, which saved the church from demolition and created the world's first museum of this kind. Inside there are enough tool collections and gardening artefacts to keep even Charlie Dimmock amused. Notice too the beautiful,

---

**WHAT TO LOOK FOR**　　　ⓘ

In the porch of St Mary-at-Lambeth Church is an unusual memorial to a man who was struck by lightning in the 18th century. He used to work in the salt house. His unfortunate end is graphically described: 'his intestines spilled out...'

Walk 15

stained-glass windows. At the rear, the peaceful 17th-century garden is scented throughout the year and there are pots of herbs for sale. We have the Tradescant family to thank for introducing many of the plants and trees seen in this country today. John Tradescant and his son were gardeners to Charles I and also adventurous travellers, bringing back specimens from Russia, America and North Africa. Appropriately, their tomb lies in the churchyard garden next to another that is dedicated to William Bligh (1754–1817), the celebrated navigator more commonly known as Captain Bligh of *Mutiny on the Bounty* fame. But why is he buried here? Despite the tarnishing of his reputation by Hollywood scriptwriters (Charles Laughton's blustering character in the 1935 film bore very little resemblance to the real Bligh), one of his early nautical successes was to tranship the highly nutritious bread fruit plant from the South Pacific to the West Indies. This provided plantation owners a reliable and cost-effective source of food for their slaves and labourers.

Back at the entrance to the church, turn left and follow the wall to **St Mary's Gardens** with its central water fountain. Continue for 100yds (91m) and turn left through an alley into the **Archbishop's Park**. Follow the tarmac path ahead, the

**Lambeth Millennium Pathway**, and notice the plaques beneath your feet. One commemorates Clapham Rovers winning the FA Cup in 1880 and another celebrates the time when the Lambeth Walk became a dance craze in 1936.

Follow the path around the tennis courts and past a children's playground, to leave the park opposite St Thomas's Hospital. Turn right and cross Royal Street – look for the London Eye peeping above the hospital. Cross **Lambeth Palace Road** then, at the junction, turn left towards the **Houses of Parliament** on the north side of Westminster Bridge.

At the Houses of Parliament turn left into **Millbank** (which used to be known as Margaret Street). A few paces beyond the statue of Oliver Cromwell turn left into **Victoria Tower Gardens**. Now follow the **Silver Jubilee Walkway**, past the sculpture by Auguste Rodin, towards the river. The six figures depict citizens of Calais who offered themselves as hostages to Edward III, who had besieged the town in 1347.

Walk up the steps at the end of the park and over the zebra crossing. Continue along the Thames Path to **Vauxhall Bridge**. Cross the bridge back to the start of the walk.

# Grace and Favour in Norwood

*Pass the tombstone of a revered cricketer before visiting South Norwood Country Park.*

| | |
|---|---|
| •DISTANCE• | 2¼ miles (3.6km) |
| •MINIMUM TIME• | 1hr 30min |
| •ASCENT / GRADIENT• | 49ft (15m) ▲▲▲ |
| •LEVEL OF DIFFICULTY• | 林林 林林 林 |
| •PATHS• | Tarmac with some rough tracks that can get muddy |
| •LANDSCAPE• | Mainly open meadows |
| •SUGGESTED MAP• | aqua3 OS Explorer 161 London South |
| •START / FINISH• | Grid reference: TQ 354689; W G Grace pub by Birkbeck Tramlink |
| •DOG FRIENDLINESS• | No problems |
| •PARKING• | In pub car park or adjacent roads |
| •PUBLIC TOILETS• | None on route |

## BACKGROUND TO THE WALK

Even if you're not a fan of the sport, the South Norwood Country Park is well worth a visit for its delightful paths (some of which run alongside a stream and a lake) and for its prolific bird life. But most people come here because of W G Grace, the man who probably did more for the game of cricket in his lifetime than any other. As well as Grace's tomb, the Victorian cemetery contains some other angelic tombstones. It's also the resting place of Frederick Wolsey, who invented the sheep-shearing machine.

**Days of Grace**

William Gilbert Grace, or 'W G' as he became known, was born in Bristol in 1848. He first began playing cricket at the age of 16 before training to become a doctor. He was a good, all-round sportsman; he also played golf and bowls but it was cricket that made him a national hero. He was such a keen player that, after visiting a house where two children were in bed with a fever, it is said that he told the mother to call him again if their combined temperatures reached two hundred and ten for two!

However, he was never a professional player, despite his incredible record for promoting the game of cricket. He played for Gloucestershire for many years before moving to south east London. His scores could be seen as even more remarkable considering the state of the pitches in the 19th century compared with the ones of today.

**Outstanding Innings**

In an era when a batsman scoring 100 runs in a single innings was a comparatively rare event, Grace scored 2,739 first class runs in 1871 and he dominated the game for more than 20 years. As well as exceptional stamina, he had an ability to see the ball early and judge its length. He was the first player in modern cricket to score two centuries in the same match. At the Oval in 1878 he threw a cricket ball more than 116yds (106m) and on his test debut there in 1880 he made 152 runs. Even at the age of 46 he scored over 1,000 runs in a season. Grace was also a formidable figure: athletic in his earlier years, he had a very high front elbow and was an excellent fielder, making 887 catches, the second highest number taken by anyone in their career.

**Sixty Not Out**

Although Grace stopped playing first-class cricket in 1908 – in his sixtieth year – he continued to play in less-important matches. During his very last match, in 1914, he managed to score 69 runs with the bat and was not out. He died from heart failure at his home in Eltham the following year. Marking the 75th anniversary of his death, journalist Christopher Martin-Jenkins said: 'W G paved the way for the golden age… the hallmark of which was the beauty and brilliance of the batting, and especially the amateur batting'.

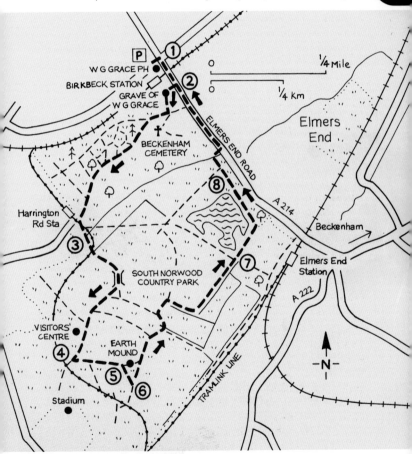

① From the **W G Grace** pub in **Witham Road** turn right. Continue past the Tramlink bridge and the

entrance to **Birkbeck Station** before turning right into **Beckenham Cemetery**.

② After the cemetery's office turn right along a path that later swings to the left. Take the left fork and then a right-hand branch to reach the grave of W G Grace. Look out for his large white marble tombstone 50yds (46m) on the left. Carry on towards the chapel ahead, turn right to join the main path and continue through the cemetery.

③ At the end of this tarmac drive go through the cemetery gates and cross the Tramlink line. Turn left along a footpath that crosses the Tramlink line again before entering **South Norwood Country Park**. Turn right after a footbridge then, at a T-junction, keep ahead and stay on this wide track past a visitors' centre.

> ### WHERE TO EAT AND DRINK ℹ️
> Only a tram line separates the grave of W G Grace from the pub bearing his name. The modern **W G Grace** pub contains memorabilia including bats and stumps and resembles a cricket pavilion from the outside. Inside is a long bar from which bar snacks are available. If only it had a lawn outside instead of a road, this would be a cricketer's paradise.

④ Just before another Tramlink level crossing, turn left to join a public footpath. Follow this as it runs parallel to the tram line.

⑤ Turn left at a fork leading to the top of the earth mound. (From the top you can see Crystal Palace, Shooter's Hill and Croydon.) To continue, turn right, downhill to rejoin the path and walk down some steps.

⑥ Turn left before the next set of steps and carry on ahead, ignoring small side paths, until you reach a

> ### WHAT TO LOOK FOR ℹ️
> South Norwood Country Park is quite flat and allows a good view of the **bird life**. Reed and sedge warblers breed here, and red kites and woodpeckers can also be found. Reed warblers arrive in mid-April to May and depart to sub-Saharan regions in August to October. Males arrive at the breeding area two weeks before the females. Unmated males trying to attract females sing at high intensity, so listen out for their long song phrases.

left-hand fork. Keep ahead, over the crossing of paths, and follow the long, straight path with drainage ditches on each side.

⑦ At the end, before the Tramlink line, go over a footbridge, then turn left and continue along the path beside a stream. Just after the path swings to the left is a five-path junction. Turn right and cross the bridge. Ignoring the first path on the left, continue as the path bends and take the left path leading to a jetty overlooking the lake.

⑧ Continue along the path and turn right along another path to leave the park. Turn left along **Elmers End Road**, past Birkbeck Tramlink, to reach the pub from where the walk began.

> ### WHILE YOU'RE THERE ℹ️
> Some of the walk follows the **Country Park Trim Trail**, a series of wooden structures where you can exercise different muscle groups. A sign next to each one describes the exercises and advises how many repetitions to do, depending on your level of fitness. These include parallel wooden bars for arm dips and another set for abdominal sit-ups.

# The Flaming City

*A linear walk tracing the route of the Great Fire of 1666, an event that created a demand for new furniture.*

| | |
|---|---|
| •DISTANCE• | 2¼ miles (3.6km) |
| •MINIMUM TIME• | 2hrs |
| •ASCENT / GRADIENT• | Negligible |
| •LEVEL OF DIFFICULTY• | |
| •PATHS• | Paved streets |
| •LANDSCAPE• | Alleys and roads in busy City of London |
| •SUGGESTED MAP• | AA Street by Street London |
| •START• | Monument tube |
| •FINISH• | Farringdon tube |
| •DOG FRIENDLINESS• | Not a good one for dogs |
| •PUBLIC TOILETS• | Monument, Mansion House |

## BACKGROUND TO THE WALK

Londoners in the 17th century must have wondered what had hit them when, within months of fighting off the Great Plague, a fire of monumental proportions began at a bakery in Pudding Lane. It was 2AM in the morning on 2 September 1666 when the baker discovered the fire. He escaped to safety along a roof, but his young assistant was not so lucky. Neither were the 13,000 houses, 87 churches and 40 livery halls that perished in the flames but, incredibly, only eight people lost their lives, although how many later died after being left homeless is unknown. It took five days to contain the fire, partly because of the high number of houses with timber roofs and the rudimentary fire-fighting equipment available at the time.

### Cabinet Decision

The event at least offered an opportunity to give the City a facelift but, due to the sheer cost and to property rights, most of the rebuilding followed the original street lines. It did, however, create a safer, more sanitary capital than before, and with the new houses came a demand for new furniture, which was excellent news for cabinet-makers.

### Rebuilding the Home

Within six years the City had been rebuilt, its boundaries extended and London was in the midst of an economic boom. By 1700 the population had increased five-fold to 500,000 inhabitants and, in terms of technical development, the city's manufacture of chests and cabinets led the way. Perhaps one of the most common items produced by a cabinet-maker was the table, candlestands and mirror ensemble, which had been introduced from France and soon became a standard item of furniture in many English homes. Cabinets were made by skilled craftsmen and therefore more expensive. However, the same techniques were later used for chests of drawers. To meet heavy demands furniture was, for the first time, offered across a range of quality and price.

Brisk trade with North America, the East Indies, East India and the Far East introduced new styles such as lacquer-ware. Although France led the way in furniture design, Oriental items such as screens were very popular. Most Londoners made do with 'japanned' furniture that was varnished in a cheaper imitation of lacquer, many of which survive today. Cane chairs too, were introduced from the Far East and most middle class homes had one or more of these so-called 'English chairs'. With the demand for furniture of all types and to match all pockets, the working life of a tradesman in the late 1600s was a happy one indeed.

## Walk 17 Directions

① Take the **Fish Street Hill** exit from the tube station and bear right towards the **Monument**. Then follow the cobbled street for 20yds

(18m) to see the plaque that marks the spot on the corner of **Pudding Lane** where the ill-fated bakery once stood. Bear right, then cross **Lower Thames Street** at the pedestrian crossing to reach **St Magnus the Martyr Church**.

**Walk 17**

② A few paces further to the right of the church, climb a set of steps and, ignoring the first exit, continue to arrive on the west side of **London Bridge**. Continue ahead, away from the river, along **King William Street** and shortly turn left along **Arthur Street** and then sharp right into **Martin Lane**, past the Olde Wine Shades. At the end turn left into **Cannon Street**. (For a detour to see the red brick houses that survived the fire, turn next left into Laurence Poultney Hill.)

**WHILE YOU'RE THERE** ⓘ
Head for the Museum of London in nearby London Wall to find out more about the Great Fire and the devastation witnessed by Samuel Pepys. This is the world's largest urban history museum – it offers an insight into London life from the Roman era to the 18th century. Many artefacts are on display, including a tiny crucifix delicately carved from bone by an inmate of Newgate Prison.

③ Cross the road and turn right into **Abchurch Lane**. At the end bear left along **King William Street** towards Bank tube station. Keep to the left, past the front of Mansion House, and notice the street on the left, Walbrook: this is the site of one of Wren's finest churches, St Stephen Walbrook Church. Turn left into **Queen Victoria Street**.

④ Continue ahead, then turn right into **Bow Lane**, past St Mary Aldermary and a row of shops, to St Mary-le-Bow at the end. Turn left into **Cheapside** which, despite being the widest road in the City, also went up in flames.

⑤ Cross this road, turn right into **Wood Street** and take the narrow alley on the right, **Milk Street**. Follow it round to enter a courtyard

**WHERE TO EAT AND DRINK** ⓘ
The culinary highlight of this walk has to be the **Place Below**, a restaurant in the crypt of St Mary-le-Bow Church. It's very popular with discerning City workers for its mouth-watering vegetarian menu. If you arrive before midday, not only do you avoid the rush but the food is cheaper too.

with an eerie entrance to the old debtors' prison. Carry on through the alley, to the left of the **Hole in the Wall** pub, to rejoin Wood Street.

⑥ Cross the road into **Goldsmith Street** and, at the Saddlers Hall opposite, turn left and rejoin **Cheapside**. Turn right and cross the pedestrian crossing to St Paul's Cathedral. Walk through the churchyard, bear left to reach **Ludgate Hill** and turn left.

⑦ Turn right and right again into **Ava Maria Lane**, which becomes **Warwick Lane**. At the end turn left along **Newgate Street**. At the traffic lights turn right along **Giltspur Street**, then left into **Cock Lane**.

⑧ Where another road meets it, turn right along **Snow Hill Lane**, past an angular building, and continue along **Farringdon Road**. At the traffic lights turn right, to reach **Farringdon tube**, where the walk ends.

**WHAT TO LOOK FOR** ⓘ
The statue on the building at the corner of Cock Lane of the 'Golden Boy' marks the spot where the fire is thought to have ended. On this site, until 1910, stood a pub called The Fortune of War where body-snatchers would leave bodies on benches and wait to hear from the surgeons of the nearby St Bartholomew's Hospital.

# Bridging the Gap

*A walk along the South Bank, tracing the history of its bridges and highlighting the buildings in between.*

| | |
|---|---|
| •DISTANCE• | 2¾ miles (4.4km) |
| •MINIMUM TIME• | 1hr 15min |
| •ASCENT / GRADIENT• | Negligible |
| •LEVEL OF DIFFICULTY• | |
| •PATHS• | Paved streets |
| •LANDSCAPE• | Riverside walk |
| •SUGGESTED MAP• | aqua3 OS Explorer 173 London North |
| •START / FINISH• | Grid reference TQ302796; Westminster tube |
| •DOG FRIENDLINESS• | On lead |
| •PUBLIC TOILETS• | North side of Blackfriars Bridge |

## BACKGROUND TO THE WALK

This is a well-trodden route and a favourite for many people as it exudes a sense of space in an otherwise highly-populated city. Long before the Romans arrived, the river was used as a highway by seafaring traders. The Italians, delighted by its potential, built the first timber bridge in AD 50. By the Middle Ages the river had become so polluted that it constituted a serious hygiene problem – it's no surprise that conditions provided the breeding ground for the Black Death, which arrived in 1348 carried by rats on ships from Europe. With such a colourful history, no wonder it's endearingly called Old Father Thames.

### Beside the Arches
Westminster may have been the bridge that opened up the South Bank but it was far from being a smooth operation. Initially built from stone in the 1740s, its opening was delayed by sabotage from ferrymen and the death of its sponsor. The Gothic patterns seen on the decorative wrought-iron bridge today are the work of Charles Barry, the Parliament architect, when the bridge was rebuilt in 1853.

In contrast, Hungerford, the only combined rail and foot crossing, was built as a suspension bridge and bought in 1859 to extend the railway line to Charing Cross station. Its legacy lives on in the West Country, for the Clifton Bridge in Bristol was constructed from the recycled, original Hungerford Bridge.

### Surreal Nostalgia
When work began to replace the original Waterloo Bridge in 1939, the Second World War was looming on the horizon. The new bridge eventually opened six years later, having been built mainly by women. Its architect, Sir Giles Gilbert Scott, was also the designer behind the popular red telephone kiosk and Bankside power station, now the impressive Tate Modern. Another building with power station roots is the Oxo Wharf, which was acquired in the 1920s by the Meat Extract Company that made the Oxo cubes still available from supermarkets today. The art deco Oxo Tower has 10ft (3m) windows, which, at night, are illuminated in such a way as to spell out the distinctive 'noughts and crosses' in red neon lights to all four corners of London.

Blackfriars, the final bridge along this stretch known as the South Bank, opened in 1769 and was originally named after the Tory Prime Minister, William Pitt – it didn't take long to change the name, though. The present construction has five cast-iron arches. The remains of the rail bridge that once ran parallel look almost surreal, like the posts of a cochineal-tinted wedding cake rising out of the water – well, I did say it was surreal.

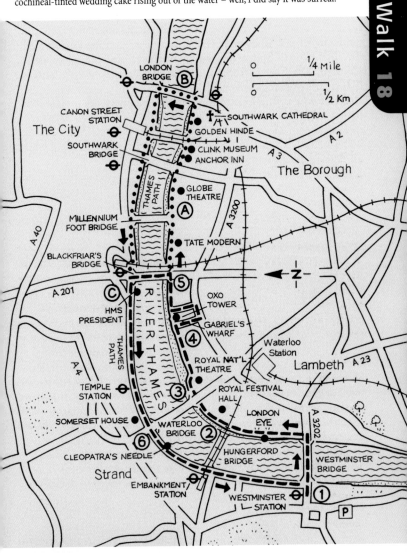

## Walk 18 Directions

① Leave **Westminster underground station** by Exit 1 to follow signs to **Westminster Pier**. Walk up the steps to your right and cross **Westminster Bridge**. Turn left along the riverfront. Ahead are the 32 transparent pods of the 2,100 ton London Eye, a huge modern ferris wheel. Just past **Jubilee Gardens**, on the right, is the next bridge, Hungerford.

Walk 18

② Continue ahead past the **Royal Festival Hall** and look to the opposite bank of the Thames for a glimpse of Cleopatra's Needle. After the National Film Theatre and its outdoor café is **Waterloo Bridge**.

③ The path bends to the right, past the Royal National Theatre and the Hayward Gallery, before reaching the craft shops and restaurants of **Gabriel's Wharf**. Turn right at the Riviera restaurant and walk through the central path lined on either side with a series of wooden sculptures. Turn left at the end into **Stamford Street** and 100yds (91m) further on take another left turn into **Barge House Street**.

### WHILE YOU'RE THERE ℹ
London Frogtours is a novel, 80 minute experience in a bright yellow amphibious craft that splashes down into the river at the Albert Embankment (although why it's not bright green is anyone's guess). Turn right at the London Eye and walk for about 100yds (91m) into Belvedere Road for departures.

④ Ahead, the brown brickwork of the **Oxo Wharf** somewhat shrouds the entrance to the Oxo Tower. Enter the glass doors to your left and catch the escalator to the eighth floor for a better view of the skyline, or continue along the ground floor to the riverside exit.

⑤ Cross **Blackfriars Bridge** and turn left to follow the **Thames Path** along the wide pavement adjacent to the river. The first boat you will pass on your left is the HMS *President*. The next set of buildings to your right after Temple tube station belong to the University of London. Immediately after these comes majestic **Somerset House**.

### WHAT TO LOOK FOR ℹ
Gabriel's Wharf was once the site of the **Eldorado Ice Cream Company**. Some 13 acres (5.3ha) in the area were saved from development into office buildings by the Coin Street Community Builders, an association formed in 1984 to create a better community environment. Here you can see some of the 160 box-style houses built in Upper Ground.

⑥ A further 200yds (183m) ahead the path passes **Cleopatra's Needle** before reaching Embankment tube. **Northumberland Avenue** is the next road to appear on your right. About 200yds (183m) further on is **Horse Guards Avenue**, which is sandwiched between the formidable buildings of the Old War Office and the Ministry of Defence. You are now almost parallel with the London Eye, on the opposite bank of the River Thames. When you reach **Westminster Bridge** turn right into **Bridge Street**, to **Westminster tube** and the start.

### WHERE TO EAT AND DRINK ℹ
Sarni's in Gabriel's Wharf serves good hot chocolate, coffee and, unsurprisingly, sandwiches. There's outside seating only, so if you're after somewhere warmer try **EAT** on the ground floor of the Oxo Tower. Just before Cannon Street Rail Bridge (on Walk 19) is the 17th-century **Anchor Inn**. It's thought that Samuel Pepys watched the Great Fire of London in 1666 from here. A spit-and-sawdust sort of place with creaking floors, it has a wide range of dishes including a good value, pre-theatre menu.

# And on to Bankside

*Continue along the River Thames and discover more about Southwark's colourful past.*
**See map and information panel for Walk 18**

| | |
|---|---|
| •DISTANCE• | 4½ miles (7.2km) |
| •MINIMUM TIME• | 2hrs 30min |
| •ASCENT / GRADIENT• | Negligible ▲▲▲ |
| •LEVEL OF DIFFICULTY• | 👫 👫 👫 |

## Walk 19 Directions (Walk 18 option)

To take this additional loop to the South Bank continue straight ahead at Point ⑤ instead of crossing Blackfriars Bridge. The awesome ex-power station on your right was made with 4 million bricks. It is now home to one of the world's most popular art galleries, Tate Modern. If this is the only stop you make it will undoubtedly be a worthwhile one.

The Millennium Foot Bridge, a few paces ahead, will go down in history as being the first pedestrian bridge to be built over the Thames for 100 years, and then immediately closed to correct a 'wobble'. But, with or without a wobble, this is a far cry from the scene in the 1100s when the area, owned by the Bishops of Winchester, was a red light district possessing 22 brothels.

Continue past the **Millennium Foot Bridge** and descend the steps on your right, crossing the road to the next building on your right, **Shakespeare's Globe** (Point Ⓐ). Performances are held here from May until September.

Beyond this is **Southwark Bridge** and, 200yds (183m) further on, **Cannon Street Rail Bridge**. A few paces on and you will pass the **Clink Museum**, on the site of the notorious old prison. Inside you'll find torture devices and a long, metal 'thief catcher' from which 'the long arm of the law' gets its name. A few paces further on are the remnants of the Bishops' Palace – sadly just a 14th-century rose window, carved in Reigate stone, and very little else.

The path winds slightly and, after 35yds (32m), leads to a full-sized replica of Sir Francis Drake's 16th-century ship, the *Golden Hinde*, which is now sandwiched among the office blocks.

A few paces further on you'll find **Southwark Cathedral**. Some of the building dates from 1220. If you time it correctly, arriving for the weekday 5.30PM service, you will hear the dulcet tones of its fine Gothic choir.

Cross **London Bridge** (Point Ⓑ), and descend the steps on the far side, following signs for the Thames Path (West). Continue along to **Blackfriars Bridge** and rejoin Walk 18 at Point Ⓒ.

# The Young Ones of Bloomsbury

*A look at Bloomsbury on a short walk, easily managed by children accompanied by adults.*

**Walk 20**

| | |
|---|---|
| •DISTANCE• | 1¼ miles (2km) |
| •MINIMUM TIME• | 1hrs |
| •ASCENT / GRADIENT• | Negligible |
| •LEVEL OF DIFFICULTY• | |
| •PATHS• | Paved streets |
| •LANDSCAPE• | Georgian houses and garden squares |
| •SUGGESTED MAP• | AA Street by Street London |
| •START• | Russell Square tube |
| •FINISH• | Holborn tube |
| •DOG FRIENDLINESS• | Not allowed in Coram Fields |
| •PUBLIC TOILETS• | None on route |

## Walk 20 **Directions**

From **Russell Square tube**, turn right and cross the road, then turn left along **Hunter Street** and past the Brunswick Shopping Centre.

The road on the right opposite the Renoir Cinema leads to a statue of Captain Thomas Coram, a sea captain who established a foundling hospital for the 'education and maintenance of exposed and deserted young children' to address the huge number of abandoned babies and children found on the streets of London. The first children were admitted into a temporary house near Hatton Garden in 1741 and transferred when the present site of 56 acres (23ha), belonging to the Earl of Salisbury, was found. To publicise his new charity, Coram persuaded his friend William Hogarth to ask British artists to donate some of their works to the hospital. It clearly worked for the

charity, thought to be the oldest in this country, is now called Coram Family and owns some important works of art that have never been bought or sold, including paintings by Hogarth, Gainsborough and Reynolds. The philanthropist Thomas Coram died in 1751 at the ripe old age of 83.

> **WHERE TO EAT AND DRINK**
> Plenty to choose from here, including the **outdoor café** in Red Lion Square. The food in **Sid's Café** in Lamb's Conduit Street is simple and hearty and the cosy place is child-friendly. If you haven't got any children with you, take a look inside the **Lamb** pub to see the original Victorian snob screens around the bar.

Continue along Hunter Street and then turn right into **Handel Street**. Follow the path through the gates to **St George's Gardens**, past the gravestones lining the walls, to leave by the gate on the right-hand side. After about 75yds (69m) turn right into **Mecklenburgh Street** and its elegant Georgian houses. Go past the private square and **Coram Fields** on your right to continue to the crossroads.

To visit **Dickens House Museum** carry on along **Doughty Street**; otherwise turn right along **Guilford Street**, and take a look at the very quaint Doughty Mews, which is the next road you'll pass. Continue along Guilford Street until you reach a statue in the middle of Guilford Place. You'll turn left along this road, which becomes **Lamb's Conduit Street** but first, notice the entrance to **Coram's Fields** on the other side of the road. A sign at the entrance says: 'Adults may only enter if accompanied by a child'. I waited for a few minutes and quizzed a man who was entering alone. 'Ah, but I work here,' he mused, as I stood peering through the gates. So the moral of this tale is take along a child if you want to visit the park and playground and a small city farm.

Back along the oddly-named **Lamb's Conduit Street**, you will pass **Great Ormond Street**, which is where you'll find the Great Ormond Street Hospital for Sick Children. Dickens, whose work was hugely popular with the lower middle classes, raised many social issues. Having been brought up to be a gentleman, it must have come as a terrible shock when his father was sent to Marshalsea debtors' prison

and 12 year old Charles was sent to work in a blacking factory. He must have worked with a fair number of street urchins and later characterised them in *Oliver Twist* (1837–8) and *David Copperfield* (1849–50). Dickens was also a fan of Great Ormond Street Hospital and raised money for it at talks and public readings. Another fan was J M Barrie, the creator of Peter Pan, who requested that the royalties went to this hospital. When this arrangement legally expired in 1988, the copyright law was changed so that the hospital continued to receive money (including an estimated $½ million from Steven Spielberg's 1991 film, *Hook*). Barrie popularised the name Wendy after speaking to a child called Margaret who, because she couldn't pronounce her 'r's, referred to him as her 'fwiendy'. Although Margaret died when she was only six years old, Barrie immortalised her as his Peter Pan heroine, Wendy.

Continue ahead, past **Dombey Street**. At the end of Lamb's Conduit Street turn right along the main road. Cross this at the pedestrian lights and turn left into **Old North Street**. This leads to **Red Lion Square**. At the other end and leave through the gates and bear right. Turn left into **Drake Procter Street** and continue until you reach the traffic lights. Cross the road and bear right to reach **Holborn tube**, where the walk ends.

---

**WHILE YOU'RE THERE** ⓘ

Charles Dickens and his wife lived at 48 Doughty Street for two years. The **museum**, which opened in 1925, is a testament to his life and works. It's also the only London home of his that is still standing. The rooms in this 'frightfully first-class family mansion', as Dickens described it, contain some of his original manuscripts, his desk and even a tiny window from an attic room in Camden Town where he once lived. He preferred to write with a goose-feather quill that had had most of its feathers removed and there are quills and ink for you to try, under supervision – but it's not easy.

# From Mayfair with Love

*A leisurely walk through wealthy Mayfair in the style of James Bond.*

| | |
|---|---|
| •DISTANCE• | 2¾ miles (4.4km) |
| •MINIMUM TIME• | 1hr 30 |
| •ASCENT / GRADIENT• | Negligible ▲▲▲ |
| •LEVEL OF DIFFICULTY• | 🚶 🚶 🚶 |
| •PATHS• | Paved streets |
| •LANDSCAPE• | Shopping, residential and business district of West End |
| •SUGGESTED MAP• | AA Street by Street London |
| •START / FINISH• | Bond Street tube |
| •DOG FRIENDLINESS• | 007 would leave his at home |
| •PUBLIC TOILETS• | None on route |

## BACKGROUND TO THE WALK

When the author Ian Fleming created the character James Bond he paved the way for a small minority of actors to participate in an adventure that would take them to some of the world's most exotic locations. Fleming's first novel, *Casino Royale*, published in 1953, introduced the tough, romantic, handsome hero who became affectionately known as 007. Fifty years on, films that are based on his books are still being made. This walk captures some of the glamour of James Bond but you must go armed with a good imagination.

### On Her Majesty's Secret Service

Mayfair was developed in the 18th century, predominantly by the wealthy Grosvenor family. It is one of the most elegant areas in London. Many of its exclusive shops bear coats of arms, denoting that they are official suppliers to the royal family, and the locality is peppered with superb hotels and restaurants – this is the type of place in which 007 would feel quite at home. In fact 'home' could be Albany, a covert block of bachelors' apartments. It was created from a townhouse owned by George III's son, who was popularised in the nursery rhyme 'the grand old Duke of York'. Byron was one of the first men to live at Albany, which has its own quiet courtyard just off Piccadilly. From here 007 would visit Old Bond Street and its cluster of exclusive shops selling jewellery (Tiffany and Cartier) and pens (Mont Blanc) and also South Audley Street, for this is where the royal gunmaker Purdey's, is to be found. A few doors away, the Spy Shop is where Q might have spent many a fine hour. He may have recommended the recording briefcase with concealed microphones that optionally transmits conversation, or perhaps the body wires or transmitting pens and calculators from this shop that sells 'business tools built to military specification'.

### License to Thrill

For relaxation, 007 could head for the Elemis Day Spa. There, for an hour or so, he would be transported to a world of sensory heaven in either the Thai, Moorish or Balinese suites, for some serious cleansing and massage in exotic surroundings. Feeling refreshed, he may then even stop off at the Kenneth Turner flower shop in Avery Row and treat the long-suffering Miss Moneypenny to an artistic bouquet. Then, assuming he was not on a case, off he'd go to Claridge's hotel in search of his favourite tipple. Now, depending upon which Bond we're talking about, this can differ, so let's stick with my favourite, Roger Moore, who played Bond in seven films. Although we all know the line: 'medium-dry martini, shaken, not stirred' Moore as 007 was in fact a champagne and wine man, and drank only three vodka martinis compared with 22 glasses of champagne and wine in his films. But don't let that put you off, for if you're following in the footsteps of 007, apart from never saying never again, how can you go to Claridge's Bar and not order such a legendary cocktail?

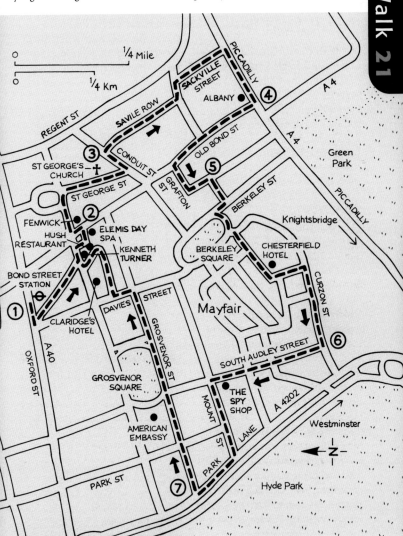

## Walk 21 Directions

① Turn left outside the tube station and sharp left into pedestrianised **South Molton Street**. At the end

turn left into **Brook Street**. Cross the road and go along the cobbled right-hand alley, **Lancashire Court**, which opens into a courtyard. A few paces past **Hush** restaurant you'll find the **Elemis Day Spa**.

Walk 21

② Turn left here and cross the road to reach the store, Fenwick. Turn right along **Brook Street** to reach **Hanover Square**. At the statue of the young William Pitt turn right into **St George Street**, past St George's Church and left at the end into **Conduit Street**.

③ Take the next right into the road of fine suits, **Savile Row**. At the end bear left and then right into **Sackville Street**. Turn right along **Piccadilly** and look out for the entrance to **Albany**'s courtyard.

---

**WHAT TO LOOK FOR**   ⓘ

**Decadence** – while you might not see many Aston Martins there will be plenty of Mercedes, BMWs and Audis. Similarly, the shops in this area of London are some of the most exclusive in the city. Enter these and you'll have the door opened for you by a man in a dark suit.

---

④ Just past the auspicious-looking Burlington Arcade turn right into **Old Bond Street** and past several exclusive shops including those of Cartier, Mont Blanc and Tiffany. Turn left after Asprey & Garrard into **Grafton Street**; which takes a 90-degree left bend, becoming **Dover Street**.

⑤ Turn right along **Hay Hill** and then right again towards Berkeley Square, crossing two zebra crossings with the square on your right, to reach handsome **Charles Street**. Beyond the Chesterfield Hotel turn left along **Queen Street** and then right into **Curzon Street**.

⑥ Turn right into **South Audley Street** and its Spy Shop, then, at Purdey's (gunmakers), turn left into **Mount Street**. At the end turn right along **Park Lane**, past the Grosvenor House Hotel.

⑦ Turn right into **Upper Grosvenor Street**, past the American Embassy on Grosvenor Square, then turn left into **Davies Street**. Next, take the first right into **Brooks Mews** and go left along the narrow Avery Row. This brings you on to **Brook Street**. From here you can retrace your steps along **South Molton Street**, back to **Bond Street tube** from where the walk began.

---

**WHILE YOU'RE THERE**   ⓘ

The **Elemis Day Spa** is a little piece of heaven in Mayfair, and the perfect place to pass an hour or two before or after the walk. The Moorish Suite is so realistic that it could be straight out of a film set.

---

**WHERE TO EAT AND DRINK**   ⓘ

First stop for 007 might be **Hush**, a smart restaurant in Lancashire Court with outside seating, that is part-owned by Geoffrey Moore, son of 007 Roger. If time is short, or you just want a hot drink, try the minimalist, modern **Carluccio's Café** in the basement of Fenwick. It has good lasagne and a choice of set menus. But for the ultimate 007 experience, make sure you stop for a vodka martini at **Claridge's Bar** in Brook Street.

# Legal Eagles at the Inns of Court

*Soak up the atmosphere of these hidden alleys and squares that featured in many of Dickens' novels.*

| | |
|---|---|
| •DISTANCE• | 1½ miles (2.4km) |
| •MINIMUM TIME• | 1hr 30min |
| •ASCENT / GRADIENT• | 49ft (15m) ▲ ▲ ▲ |
| •LEVEL OF DIFFICULTY• | 👫 👫 👫 |
| •PATHS• | Paved streets and some cobbled alleys |
| •LANDSCAPE• | Alleyways and buildings of architectural interest |
| •SUGGESTED MAP• | AA Street by Street London |
| •START• | Temple tube |
| •FINISH• | Holborn tube |
| •DOG FRIENDLINESS• | Not allowed in many streets |
| •PUBLIC TOILETS• | Lincoln's Inn Fields |

## BACKGROUND TO THE WALK

The compact area highlighted here between Temple and Fleet Street is home to some fine buildings that survived the Great Fire of London. Not only that, but to walk through this great legal institution is to take a step back in time. Charles Dickens, who was a keen walker and often covered 20 miles (32km) in a day, was a frequent visitor to the area and used it as the setting for some of his novels.

### Personal Experience

Born to parents who lived beyond their means, Dickens first saw the darker side of life when his father was imprisoned for debt. He went to work in a shoe-blacking factory and it was this experience that formed the basis of his views on the injustice of poverty and that broadened his scope and insight. At the age of 15 he spent a year as a solicitor's clerk in Gray's Inn. Later he mastered the art of shorthand and took a job as a reporter on the *Morning Herald* before producing a series of pieces for monthly and weekly publications, writing these under the pseudonym of 'Boz'. Dickens used his articles to highlight social issues and the plight of the poor. These short pieces also allowed Dickens to develop the technical skill that he would use to great effect later.

His novels were initially serialised in this way too and Victorian readers, especially the lower middle classes, couldn't get enough of him – they would eagerly await the next instalment, just as many people today follow 'soaps' on television.

### Living up to Expectations

You'll see when you reach Fountain Court how little it can have changed in more than 150 years. The place is particularly atmospheric at dusk when the Victorian street lamps are alight. It is here that Tom meets his sister Ruth, in the novel, *Martin Chuzzlewit* (1843): '…the fountain sparkled in the sun, and laughingly its liquid played music and merrily the idle drops of water danced and danced'.

Further on, the Middle Temple, with its winding alleys and gardens, feels like a village. Based on his time as a solicitor's clerk at Ellis and Blackmore, Dickens wrote: 'There is yet, in the Temple, something of a clerkly monkish atmosphere which public offices of law have not disturbed and even legal firms have failed to scare away…' In *Martin Chuzzlewit*, Dickens describes how Tom felt about going to work in the Temple: '… he turned his face towards an atmosphere of unaccountable fascination, as surely as he turned it to the London smoke … until the time arrived for going home again and leaving it, like a motionless cloud behind'. Although the London smoke is no longer around, you'll see what Dickens meant as you explore this little area of calm away from the busy City streets.

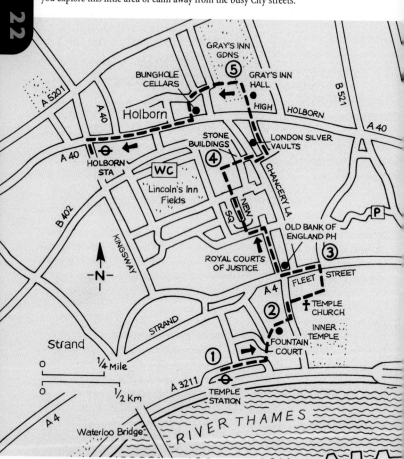

# Walk 22 **Directions**

① Turn left at the exit to **Temple tube** and up a set of steps. Turn right into **Temple Place**. At the end go left into **Milford Lane** then, after a few more paces, go up another series of steps, into **Inner Temple**.

Turn right by the Edgar Wallace pub into Devreux Court, walk under the archway and go down the steps to **Fountain Court**.

② Bear left under an archway into **Middle Temple**, past a small fountain and garden and up the steps, then bear right through some

**Walk 22**

cloisters to reach the **Temple Church**. Go through an archway to the right of the church, then left through another archway and along a cobbled alley to **Fleet Street**.

③ Turn left along Fleet Street and cross at the pedestrian lights. After the **Old Bank of England** pub turn right into **Bell Yard** and continue ahead on the path that runs alongside the Royal Courts of Justice. Turn left and then right into **New Square** and follow the avenue of trees.

④ Take the path on the far right along **Stone Buildings** and, ahead, go through the gates that lead to **Chancery Lane**. Cross this road and turn right into the street called Southampton Buildings. After just 20yds (18m) this veers sharply left, past the London Silver Vaults. Cross

**High Holborn** and pass through a gateway to Gray's Inn on the right. A few paces further, after Gray's Inn Hall, turn left into **Field Court**.

⑤ Continue to the end then turn right and go up the steps into **Jockeys Fields**. Bear left along **Bedford Row** and take the second road on the left, Hand Court. Just past the Bunghole Cellars at the end, turn right along **High Holborn** to reach **Holborn tube**.

# Walking with the Pensioners of Chelsea

*Famed for its expensive properties, Chelsea is also home to the most famous pensioners in Britain.*

| | |
|---|---|
| •DISTANCE• | 3¾ miles (6km) |
| •MINIMUM TIME• | 2hrs |
| •ASCENT / GRADIENT• | Negligible |
| •LEVEL OF DIFFICULTY• | |
| •PATHS• | Paved streets and tarmac paths |
| •LANDSCAPE• | Mainly riverside views |
| •SUGGESTED MAP• | aqua3 Explorer 161 London South |
| •START / FINISH• | Sloane Square tube |
| •DOG FRIENDLINESS• | On lead |
| •PARKING• | Difficult – best to catch tube |
| •PUBLIC TOILETS• | Royal Hospital Chelsea Museum |

## BACKGROUND TO THE WALK

Pick up any book about walking in London and you will notice one thing: the walks are either north or south of the river – surprisingly few combine both, which doesn't do much to erase the north/south divide that, as odd as it may sound, still clearly exists. So this walk includes not only those elegant streets of Chelsea but also the gratifying expanse of Battersea Park to the south.

### Keeping Up Appearances
Somewhere just off the fashionable King's Road lies a building as majestic as any you're likely to encounter. Some say it's as great as St Paul's Cathedral, and, although this is debatable, Sir Christopher Wren certainly left his mark on it. The building in question, the Royal Hospital Chelsea, was founded by Charles II and built in 1692 for veteran soldiers who had either served in the army for 20 years or been wounded. The minimum age for entry is now normally 65 and there is still accommodation for 500. Living here, the pensioner surrenders his army pension and in return receives a small room or berth, all meals (taken in the spectacular Great Hall where the Duke of Wellington lay in state before he was buried in St Paul's Cathedral), clothing and medical care.

### Hearts of Oak
Each year, on 29 May, the hospital celebrates Founder's Day. The statue of Charles II in the Centre Court is decorated with oak leaves to commemorate the time when he hid in an oak tree after escaping from the Battle of Worcester in 1651.

Chelsea Pensioners are easily recognised by their unusual three-cornered hats and their scarlet coats, adorned with military medals. It is indeed a joy to see them, both north and south of the river. Oddly the coats have become a distinguishing feature of the Pensioners' identity. They are modelled on the red coats worn by British troops from the Civil War onwards and can have changed little since the Royal Hospital's foundation.

**The Grass is Greener on the Other Side**

Before Queen Victoria came on the scene, Battersea Park, as we now know it, was merely derelict marshland with ditches full of water that flowed into the river. But, in the 19th century, Sir James Pennethorne created the 200 acre (81ha) landscape we see today. Battersea is the sort of park that has something for everyone (duels notwithstanding – the last being between the Duke of Wellington and Lord Winchelsea). In the summer months you'll hear anything from jazz music to the thud of a football, and see picnickers enjoying the sun along with joggers and cyclists. And there's also another section of the Thames Path that runs alongside the river, with views over to the Chelsea Embankment and its constant flow of traffic. But over here it's different: it's peaceful and more than just a back garden for the Chelsea set – and, if the Peace Pagoda could speak, it would probably agree.

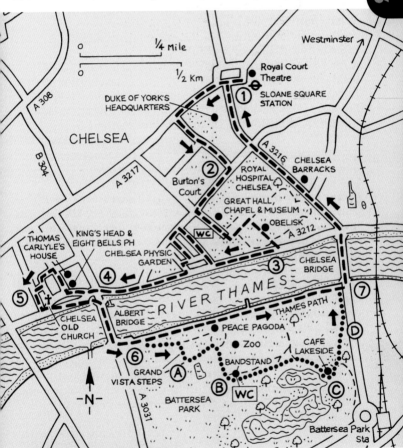

## Walk 23 **Directions**

① From **Sloane Square tube** walk ahead, crossing **Lower Sloane Street**. Go past John Lewis and, a few paces on your left, the Duke of York's Headquarters. Turn left into **Cheltenham Terrace** then bear left into **Franklin's Row**.

② Take the first right along **Royal Hospital Road**. Just beyond the lawns on the right turn left into the

**Walk 23**

hospital grounds at **Chelsea Gate**. A few paces further on the left, a gravel path leads to the Great Hall, chapel and museum. Continue to the end of the road and turn left on to some playing fields. Now head towards the obelisk, bear right and leave through the gates to the **Chelsea Embankment**.

③ Turn right along the **Embankment** and right into **Tite Street**, where Oscar Wilde once lived. At the top turn left into **Paradise Walk**. The houses in this narrow, quiet road have window boxes and roof terraces. Turn right and then sharp left towards the Embankment and walk past the **Chelsea Physic Garden**.

④ At the traffic lights cross **Oakley Street** and bear right along the narrow **Cheyne Walk**. Turn right by the quirkily-named **King's Head and Eight Bells** pub into **Cheyne Row**, where Thomas Carlyle lived. At the end turn left into **Upper Cheyne Row**. Turn left again into **Lawrence Street** – where there is a plaque to mark the Chelsea Porcelain Works – then turn right into **Justice Walk**. (Don't be fooled into thinking the sign of a red-robed judge is a pub, it merely identifies where the old courthouse used to be!)

⑤ Turn left into **Old Church Street** and at the bottom is Chelsea Old Church, with a statue outside of Thomas More, who worshipped here. Walk through **Chelsea Embankment Gardens** and cross the **Albert Bridge**.

⑥ At a 'Riverside Walk' sign turn left through the gate into **Battersea Park**. Follow the **Thames Path**, past the Peace Pagoda in the park, along to **Chelsea Bridge**.

⑦ Turn left to cross the bridge and continue ahead, passing Chelsea Barracks on the right before joining **Lower Sloane Street**. Turn right to retrace your steps back to **Sloane Square tube**.

# Simply Battersea Park

*A longer circuit through the park that became a showcase for 18th-century horticulture.*
**See map and information panel for Walk 23**

| | |
|---|---|
| •DISTANCE• | 5 miles (8km) |
| •MINIMUM TIME• | 3hrs |
| •ASCENT / GRADIENT• | Negligible  |
| •LEVEL OF DIFFICULTY• | 🚶🚶 🚶🚶 🚶 |

## Walk 24 Directions (Walk 23 option)

At Point ⑥ continue along the **Riverside Walk** but, instead of following the path ahead, take the first path on the right then, at a junction, turn left. The path joins a wide drive. After 80yds (73m) turn right down the **Grand Vista Steps** and go to the end, past the fountains, and turn left, Point Ⓐ.

Continue for 50yds (46m) and, with the **Peace Pagoda** on your left, take the path to your right. Continue until the path joins a wide drive, Point Ⓑ. Turn left, past the bandstand, along the tree-lined

---

**WHAT TO LOOK FOR** ⓘ
The **park's layout** has remained largely unchanged since the 19th century. Gardeners will be interested to learn that, during the Second World War, the park had 6,000 allotments, a pig farm and gun emplacements. Designed by the horticultural pioneer John Gibson, it featured Britain's first public sub-tropical garden. It was a showcase for diverse plants brought from around the world. A formidable sight is the **Battersea Power Station**, one of London's best-known landmarks, which remains sadly empty.

---

avenue, now heading towards a lake. At the end of this road turn right at the gates, with the lake to your right, and this will bring you to the **Café Lakeside**, Point Ⓒ.

---

**WHERE TO EAT AND DRINK** ⓘ
**Café Lakeside** has outdoor picnic tables overlooking the boating lake, from where there is a good view of the old pump house (now the information centre and modern art gallery). Food includes salads, hot dishes and there's a children's menu.

---

Continue past the café and take the first left. Cross the drive and go through the gate opposite. Follow the path by fencing on your right, cross a mound and pass an athletics track on your left, Point Ⓓ.

Continue, to follow some fencing until this path joins a tarmac one to **Chelsea Bridge**. Turn left at the main gate and walk over the bridge. Here, at Point ⑦, you rejoin the route of Walk 23.

---

**WHILE YOU'RE THERE** ⓘ
Near the athletics track, at Point Ⓓ, is a gap between a wooden fence and a path through open glades and woodland. This nature reserve, called the **Wilderness**, is home to bullfinches, long-tailed tits and robins. Beetles also live here under little mounds of woodpile.

Walk 25

# A Web of Words in Totteridge and Mill Hill

*A look at rural north London, which left a lasting impression on the editor of the Oxford English Dictionary.*

| | |
|---|---|
| •DISTANCE• | 4½ miles (7.2km) |
| •MINIMUM TIME• | 2hrs 15min |
| •ASCENT / GRADIENT• | 262ft (80m) ▲▲▲ |
| •LEVEL OF DIFFICULTY• | 🚶🚶 🚶 |
| •PATHS• | Cross-field paths, very muddy after rain |
| •LANDSCAPE• | A variety of open fields, woods and rural roads |
| •SUGGESTED MAP• | aqua3 OS Explorer 173 London North |
| •START / FINISH• | Grid reference: TQ 225928 |
| •DOG FRIENDLINESS• | Keep on lead across fields as many are farmed |
| •PARKING• | In front of Sheepwash Pond |
| •PUBLIC TOILETS• | None on route |

## Walk 25 Directions

With **Sheepwash Pond** on your left, walk along the **Ridgeway** passing the buildings of Mill Hill School on the right and a row of quaint cottages on your left.

Sir James Murray might have followed in his father's profession and become a draper were it not for his fascination for words. As a child in the 1840s he was rarely found without a book in his pocket. His belief that 'knowledge is power' led him to educate himself and get a job as a bank clerk and later, as a schoolmaster. Murray began

> **WHAT TO LOOK FOR** ⓘ
>
> **Totteridge Fields** is a nature reserve and conservation area managed by the London Wildlife Trust. This traditional lowland pastoral landscape of hay meadows is quite a rare sight and is home to wild flowers such as meadowsweet and buttercups.

teaching at Mill Hill School in 1870. Remaining there for 15 years, he considered it to be his 'golden age'. It was during this time that he was asked to edit the Oxford English Dictionary, a job that took considerably longer than anticipated and stretched him beyond belief. The task was massive and with help from a dedicated team of assistants, it took an astounding five years to reach the word 'ant'. Murray kept two tons of source quotations in his workroom, which he called the 'Scriptorium'. He left Mill Hill in 1885 for Oxford to devote more time to the project. Although he died before the dictionary was completed, Murray was still responsible for compiling at least half of the work – he set the standards and created the original model.

Continue along the **Ridgeway** as it bears left, past a long, white-timbered Quaker meeting house. Beyond the imposing Institute for

Medical Research turn left into **Burtonhole Lane**. Stay on this as it swings to the left, past Eleanor Crescent, to descend gradually. Turn left opposite Hillview Road, along a narrow path that later bends to the right and passes farmland and a nursery. When you reach the gates of Folly Farm, turn right to follow the route of **Folly Brook**.

Turn left before a gate. Follow a long path between hedgerows. Cross the stile at the end of this and head for the road, with **Long Pond** on your left. Cross **Totteridge Common**, bear right, and follow the path by a wood for 300yds (274m). Turn left into **Horseshoe Lane**, along a path signposted 'Mays Lane'. This becomes a track lined with tree cuttings as it approaches the last house, **Fairlight Cottage**.

Climb the stile and continue on a gently descending path across the left-hand edge of a field, to climb another stile near an electricity pylon. Continue ahead but turn left before a footbridge, signposted 'Dollis Valley Greenwalk'. After 100yds (91m) turn right, through the trees, across meadows.

Walk ahead, across the field and through a gate. Continue along a path beside **Dollis Brook**. Go through a double set of gates and follow the path, on the right-hand edge of a field, staying to the left of the brook. The footpath then crosses another field and passes

through another double set of gates on either side of a footbridge. Keep ahead to another gate and continue as it veers to the right along an enclosed path. When you reach a meeting of paths with a stile to your left, go through the gate on your right and up the steps. Now follow the waymarked path; it turns right along the edge of the field to reach **Hendon Wood Lane**. Turn left and, at the crossroads, join the footpath ahead through **Highwood Hill**, signposted 'Mill Hill'.

**WHERE TO EAT AND DRINK**
The best thing about the Orange Tree pub in Totteridge village is its position away from the road, overlooking a pond. That's not to say the food isn't good – the portions are large too. The lounge bar is comfortable and the beers include IPA, Worthington Best Bitter and Fuller's London Pride. Dogs must be left outside, but the chances are that, on a fine day, you'll be joining them.

Keep on the path, through a gate and bear right through **Totteridge Fields** nature reserve. Go through the gate on to the road. Turn left, along the **Ridgeway**, which soon veers to the right. After ¼ mile (400m) you'll pass the Old Mill House and what was once the village post office. To see Sunnyside, with its blue plaque indicating Murray's period of residence, turn right along **Hammers Lane**. Otherwise continue ahead for about 50yds (46m) to return to **Sheepwash Pond**.

**WHILE YOU'RE THERE**
Take a look at Sunnyside, the large, white house in Hammers Lane where James A H Murray lived for 15 years. The Murray family thought Mill Hill's ponds, old inns and rows of cottages were charming and enjoyed their time here. Murray, who was tall and thin and had a sandy-coloured beard, looked serious but he was prone to performing pranks. He once drew a life-size skeleton on black paper and hung it in the dark to scare three boarders from the school when they returned after a night out.

# Trent Park: from House Parties to Education

*A gentle stroll around Trent Country Park, where there is something for the whole family.*

| | |
|---|---|
| •DISTANCE• | 3 miles (4.8km) |
| •MINIMUM TIME• | 1hr 45min |
| •ASCENT / GRADIENT• | 230ft (70m) |
| •LEVEL OF DIFFICULTY• | |
| •PATHS• | Mainly woodland tracks |
| •LANDSCAPE• | Grasslands and woodland |
| •SUGGESTED MAP• | aqua3 OS Explorer 173 London North |
| •START / FINISH• | Grid reference: TQ 283971; Cockfosters tube ¼ mile (400m) |
| •DOG FRIENDLINESS• | Keep on lead near Pets Corner |
| •PARKING• | Trent Park car park off Cockfosters Road |
| •PUBLIC TOILETS• | At car park |

## BACKGROUND TO THE WALK

It is easy to take things for granted when you see them every week – Trent Park mansion is no exception. It is now used by the Middlesex University as part of the Trent Park campus. As a mature student in the mid-1990s I would marvel at its façade and wish my class was taking place in one of its grand rooms instead of in a nearby stable block, where I attended a weekly module before dashing off to another, less striking campus. No doubt if I'd spent more time exploring, I would have heard then about the mansion's colourful past and discovered the wonderful woodland walks.

### The Roaring Twenties

In its heyday in the 1920s, the mansion was a hub for society parties where guests included Winston Churchill, Charlie Chaplin and even T E Lawrence (of Arabia). Also, it is believed that the late Queen Mother got engaged here. Built as a small villa in 1778, Trent Park was extended when one extravagant owner, Philip Sassoon, inherited the property along with others in Bombay, Brighton and Park Lane. His father had been a merchant banker and married into the wealthy Rothschild family. Much of the brickwork is from Devonshire House in Piccadilly, which Sassoon bought, together with the window frames, when the house was demolished. He liked to impress: the obelisk in the grounds at the back of the house was erected when the Duke and Duchess of Kent visited during their honeymoon in 1934. Records show that Sassoon would order fresh fish each day from Billingsgate Fish Market to feed the 100 or so pelicans and flamingos that decorated the large lake, created when three streams on the estate were dammed.

Flowers in the house were changed twice a day and the ones in the rooms of female guests would match the colour of the dress they wore the previous evening. There was always plenty to drink – in fact 25 bottles of wine were ordered for each guest to consume over a weekend. With that amount of alcohol it's a wonder anyone could recollect the weekends at all, which might explain why only three people went to the funeral of Philip Sassoon when he died in 1939.

**Secrets and Spies**

During the Second World War the mansion was used as an interrogation centre for high-ranking German officers. Rudolf Hess was seen here after his mysterious flight to Britain in May 1941. One prisoner of war recalled being offered a glass of whisky and a cigar before chatting to a British officer for 30 minutes. Perhaps because of this relaxed approach it should not come as a complete surprise to discover that this was one of the first places to be bugged by the Germans.

## Walk 26 Directions

① Take the **London Loop path** to the left of the information board by the **café** in Trent Country Park car park. A further 400yds (366m) after the picnic tables the path swings to

the right and runs alongside a field. Continue for another 300yds (274m) and cross a footbridge over a ditch.

② At the end of the field bear left beside a hedgerow. To follow the nature trail, enter the wooden gate opposite. Otherwise, continue along the path, which then dips and rejoins a wider path 50yds (46m) ahead. A few paces further, the path bends to the right above a lake. Ignore the next path on the right and continue into the wood towards **Camlet Hill**.

③ After 100yds (91m) ignore a left fork and soon the track widens and swings gently to the right before passing the Hadley Road car park (under the trees).

---

**WHAT TO LOOK FOR** ⓘ

In early spring look out for the **daffodils** in front of the mansion, originally planted by Philip Sassoon for the visit of Stanley Baldwin, a known fan of Wordsworth's poetry. The university has recently raised funds to maintain this colourful tradition. Although you can take a walk around the grounds, the mansion is not open to the public.

---

④ Turn right at a junction and, a few paces further on, cross a track by a water tap (beware of cars heading for the car park). Follow the path through **Ride Wood**, as it runs parallel with a bridle path and Hadley Road before swinging to the right.

---

**WHERE TO EAT AND DRINK** ⓘ

**Ferny Hill Farm** in Ferny Hill, Hadley Wood has a tea room and a farm shop. Inside are neatly arranged boxes of carrots, turnips and cabbages and, on the counter, cartons of eggs. This is a wonderful hotch-potch of a place with carvings made by the local wood-turner and locally made jams for sale, as well as a selection of cards and paintings. The tea room serves the usual snacks and fresh filled baguettes.

---

⑤ Go through a kissing gate, cross a brook and go through another kissing gate. After 200yds (183m) there's a house on the left and a road; follow this for 100yds (91m).

⑥ Turn right into the Middlesex University car park and follow this to the end. Turn left into the box-hedged gardens (known as **Wisteria Walk**) and continue towards the stables and clock tower on your left. With the mansion behind you, take the path to the right, which joins a wider road leading to a gate. Bear right along this towards a column in the centre of a mini-roundabout.

---

**WHILE YOU'RE THERE** ⓘ

The **Nature Trail** is just over 1 acre (0.4ha) in size. It includes an area of hazel that was planted by a children's wildlife club ten years ago. This traditional wood was chosen because it's pliable and grows up to 12 inches (30cm) each year, so it is useful for hedge-laying. In spring the trail is carpeted in bluebells.

---

⑦ A further 50yds (46m) on is **Pets Corner** and the visitor centre with a fine selection of wooden rocking horses. Continue along this long, straight path, passing a pond on the left. Turn right along a narrow path, just before a stone monument, back to the car park where the walk began.

# My Kingdom for a Park

*A healthy, linear walk from St James's Park to Kensington Gardens.*

| | |
|---|---|
| **•DISTANCE•** | 4¼ miles (6.8km) |
| **•MINIMUM TIME•** | 2hrs 30min |
| **•ASCENT / GRADIENT•** | 66ft (20m)   ▲ ▲ ▲ |
| **•LEVEL OF DIFFICULTY•** | 🚶 🚶 🚶 |
| **•PATHS•** | Mainly tarmac paths through the parks |
| **•LANDSCAPE•** | Parkland with occasional busy road and hum of traffic |
| **•SUGGESTED MAP•** | aqua3 OS Explorer 173 London North |
| **•START•** | Grid reference TQ 303803; Charing Cross tube |
| **•FINISH•** | Grid reference TQ 255794; High Street Kensington tube |
| **•DOG FRIENDLINESS•** | On lead through gardens |
| **•PUBLIC TOILETS•** | In each park |

## BACKGROUND TO THE WALK

> 'The kiss of the sun for pardon,
> The song of the birds for mirth,
> One is nearer God's Heart in a garden,
> Than anywhere else on earth'

This short, 19th-century verse, written by Dorothy Gurney, summarises why this walk is special. Unlike some of the other, less worn routes, the Royal Parks are popular areas but surprisingly few people have visited them all – and even fewer have walked them in succession. This walk will be like reading books by different authors. You might like them all but by comparing and contrasting you will undoubtedly come out with a favourite.

### Nash to the Rescue

St James's Park, the oldest of the Royal Parks, started life rather unceremoniously as a swamp, but Henry VIII soon acquired it. By the time the Stuarts came to the throne, improvements had been made, and at one time it was even home to an exotic menagerie. It was the wish of Charles II to make it look as much like Versailles as possible. After planting trees, laying lawns and setting up an aviary, he opened it to the public. Around 150 years later the architect, John Nash, replaced the French layout with the quintessentially English one that you see today.

The contrast of Green Park may be just what's needed if you prefer a less manicured environment. It certainly lives up to its name, as there are no flowerbeds to add any other colour to this small park, which has had its fair share of duels, despite the calming surroundings. Charles II built an ice house here to cool his wines and drinks during the summer months. The adjacent Constitution Hill was named after his habit of walking 'for health'. Sensible man!

In Hyde Park there are lime trees, rose gardens and the Serpentine, a lake on which you can usually take a boat out. Kensington Gardens is on the other side of the Serpentine Bridge and here you'll pass the gates in front of Kensington Palace (where the grass was transformed into a sea of flowers after the death of Diana, Princess of Wales in 1997).

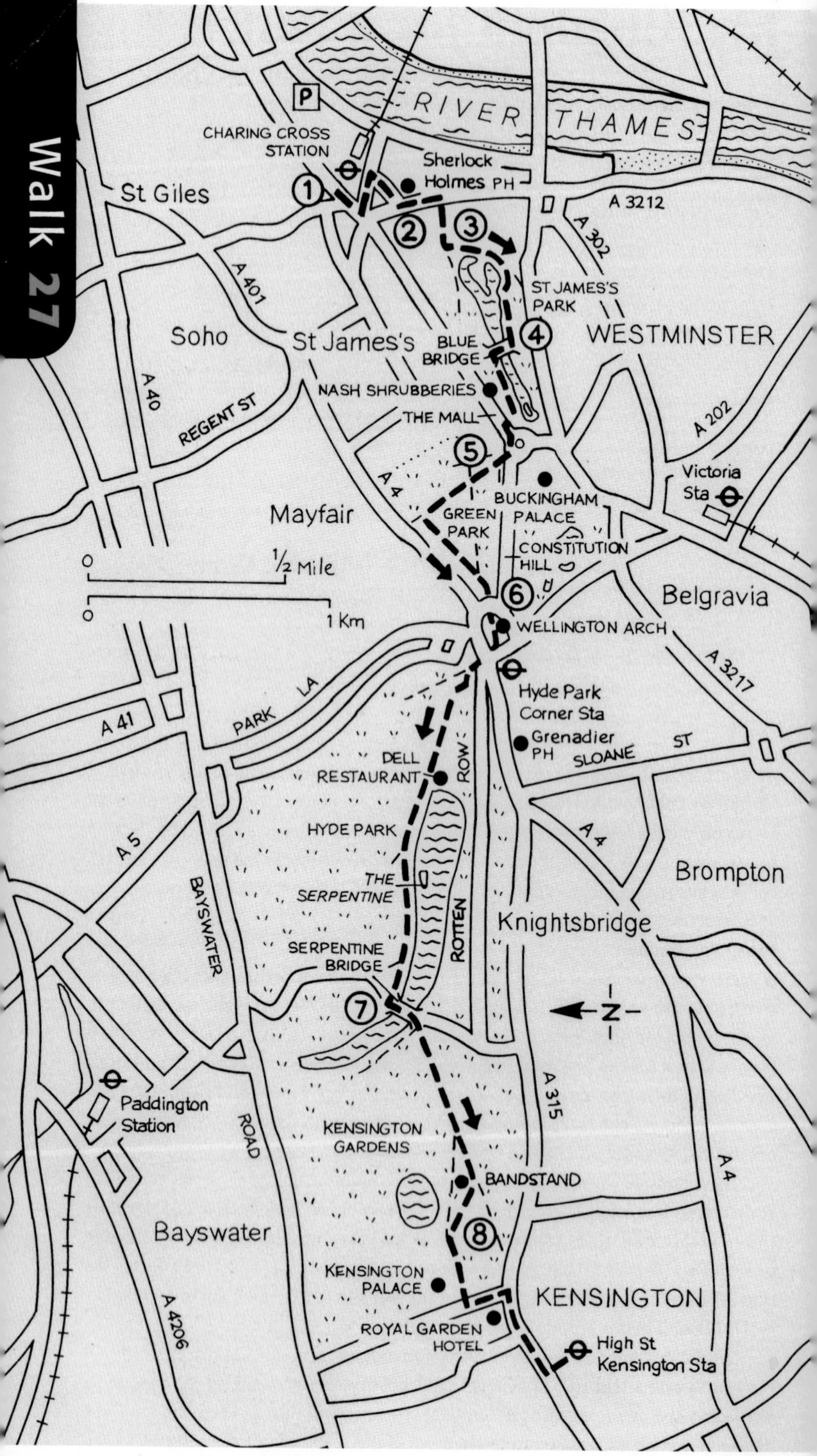

RIVER THAMES

P

CHARING CROSS
STATION

① Sherlock
Holmes PH

A 3212

St Giles

A 302

②  ③

St James's

St James's
Park

Soho

A 401

BLUE
BRIDGE

④

WESTMINSTER

REGENT ST

NASH SHRUBBERIES

A 40

THE MALL

A 202

⑤

Victoria
Sta

Mayfair

A 4

GREEN
PARK

BUCKINGHAM
PALACE

CONSTITUTION
HILL

Belgravia

½ Mile

⑥

1 Km

WELLINGTON ARCH

PARK LA

Hyde Park
Corner Sta

A 3217

A 41

DELL
RESTAURANT

ROW

Grenadier
PH    SLOANE    ST

A 5

HYDE PARK

*THE*
*SERPENTINE*

ROTTEN

A 4

Brompton

BAYSWATER

SERPENTINE
BRIDGE

Knightsbridge

⑦

←—N—→

Paddington
Station

A 315

ROAD

KENSINGTON
GARDENS

Bayswater

BANDSTAND

⑧

A 4

A 4206

KENSINGTON
PALACE

KENSINGTON

ROYAL GARDEN
HOTEL

High St
Kensington Sta

## Walk 27 **Directions**

① From **Charing Cross Station** turn left into the **Strand** and left again into **Northumberland Street**. Bear left along **Northumberland Avenue** and, after a few paces, cross into Great Scotland Yard.

② At the end turn left into **Whitehall**, cross to the other side and head for the arch of **Horse Guards Parade**, where the guards are on duty for an hour at a time. Through the arch is a gravel square used for the Beating the Retreat ceremony in June.

### WHERE TO EAT AND DRINK ⓘ
There are **cafés** in the parks. Pubs include the **Sherlock Holmes** in Northumberland Avenue, which serves its own label ale as well as Flowers and London Pride. The **Grenadier**, famed for its bloody Marys and resident ghost, is worth the short detour to Wilton Row.

③ Enter **St James's Park** to the left of the Guards Monument and follow the path that bears left around the lake, taking the first right-hand fork. Continue along this path, past weeping willow trees, to a blue bridge.

④ Cross the bridge, stopping half-way across to enjoy the views: westwards is Buckingham Palace and eastwards is Horse Guards Parade, where the skyline looks almost fairytale-like. Turn left, past the **Nash Shrubberies**, and leave the park on the right. Cross **The Mall** and enter **Green Park** from Constitution Hill.

⑤ Take the second path on the left and continue over another set of paths. At the next junction take the second path on the left. Where the next paths cross, take the left-hand path that inclines slightly to **Hyde Park Corner**.

### WHAT TO LOOK FOR ⓘ
Just across the Blue Bridge in St James's Park is an area called the **Nash Shrubberies**. It has been restored to Nash's original, 'floriferous' specifications, with an emphasis on foliage.

⑥ Use the underpass to first reach the central island and **Wellington Arch**, and then **Hyde Park** itself. Cross the road, **Rotten Row**, and follow the left-hand path through a rose garden with a cherub fountain. After 440yds (402m) follow a path to the right of the **Dell Restaurant** and continue beside the Serpentine.

⑦ Walk under the **Serpentine Bridge** and up some steps on the right. Cross the bridge and enter **Kensington Gardens**. Take the middle path and continue ahead, ignoring other paths to a bandstand, but turning right at the next opportunity.

⑧ At a junction bear left along the path that runs to the left of the gates to the Kensington Palace state apartments. At the end turn left to reach **Kensington High Street**. Pass the Royal Garden Hotel, **Kensington Church Street** and cross Kensington High Street to the **tube station** on the left.

### WHILE YOU'RE THERE ⓘ
The **views** from the 4th-floor balcony of Wellington Arch into the gardens of Buckingham Palace and along Constitution Hill are worth the small admission price alone. Arrive around 11:30AM or 12:30PM and you'll see the Household Cavalry trotting past, on their way back to their barracks.

**Walk 27**

# Spring has Sprung on Hampstead Heath

*Explore one of London's best-loved open spaces, a one-time spa and the scene of an unfortunate murder in the 1950s.*

**Walk 28**

| | |
|---|---|
| •DISTANCE• | 4¼ miles (6.8km) |
| •MINIMUM TIME• | 2hrs |
| •ASCENT / GRADIENT• | 344ft (105m) ▲▲▲ |
| •LEVEL OF DIFFICULTY• | 🏃 🏃 🏃 |
| •PATHS• | Mainly well-trodden heathland tracks |
| •LANDSCAPE• | Heath and woodland scenery and some impressive views across London |
| •SUGGESTED MAP• | aqua3 OS Explorer 173 London North |
| •START / FINISH• | Grid reference: TQ 264858; Hampstead tube |
| •DOG FRIENDLINESS• | Keep on lead near Kenwood House |
| •PARKING• | Car park off East Heath Road |
| •PUBLIC TOILETS• | Highgate |

## BACKGROUND TO THE WALK

A walk on the sprawling Heath, just 4 miles (6.4km) from central London, is the perfect escape from the pressures of city life. Hampstead first became fashionable in the 18th century, when the discovery of spring water transformed the village into a Georgian spa town. There was no stopping the writers, poets and painters who were attracted by the green, open spaces and healthy aspect. This remains the case today, although the only spring water you'll find now is that produced by the large manufacturers and sold by the bottle in shops and pubs.

### The End of an Era

Hampstead has another claim to fame or, perhaps in this case, notoriety. The village was the scene of a murder that signalled the end of capital punishment in this country. The crime was committed by Ruth Ellis, who became the last woman to be hanged in Britain. Near the end of the walk, in a road called South Hill Park, is the Magdala Tavern. Ruth Ellis was a hostess at a nightclub in Soho. During this time she had a stormy relationship with a racing driver, David Blakely. When he ended the affair Ellis first caused a disturbance outside his Hampstead flat. Two days later, as he left the Magdala Tavern, she took a gun from her handbag and shot him – he was dead on arrival at hospital. The case aroused a lot of public interest and although a newspaper paid for two defence barristers at her trial at the Old Bailey, Ellis remained adamant that she intended to kill Blakely. With no doubts about her guilt, the jury took less than 30 minutes to agree on a verdict, and the rest is history.

### Back to the Spa

Aside from that episode, Hampstead remains pretty much untainted by modern life. There are plenty of opportunities for you to wander off in to the wilder side of the Heath should you wish. Indeed, one of the delights of this area is in exploring the many pathways that criss-cross the grasslands and delve into woodland. If you use the directions as a base and decide to veer off the beaten track, you shouldn't have many problems finding your way back to the main paths.

Covering almost 800 acres (324ha), Hampstead Heath contains 25 ponds and a mixture of ancient woodland, bogs, hedgerows and grassland. Many writers seeking inspiration have discovered that this environment is the perfect antidote to writers' block. In fact, Keats had one of his most creative periods after moving to Hampstead. No doubt he was inspired by the wonderful vistas and the variety of walks that make the area so special, both to locals and to its millions of visitors each year.

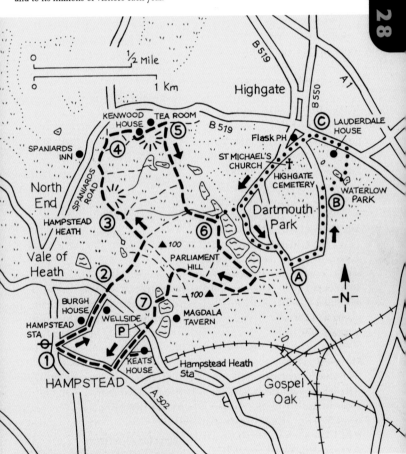

## Walk 28 **Directions**

① Turn left outside **Hampstead tube** into **Back Lane** and on into **Flask Walk**. Continue down the hill past **Burgh House** and follow **Well Walk**, passing **Wellside** on the right until it reaches **East Heath Road**.

Cross over and continue along the heath path.

② Follow a tree-lined path for 200yds (183m), as far as a junction and a water tap. Continue for a further 100yds (91m) and turn left at a bench. The track narrows and zig-zags slightly before coming to a

**Walk 28**

gate indicating the entrance to the 112 acres (45ha) maintained by English Heritage's Iveagh Bequest.

③ Bear left. The path descends gently and opens on to heathland. Follow this path to the right, on to a wider track. Pass some benches with views over to Highgate village. Continue ahead into woodland. If you have a dog, it should be on a lead now. Pass through a wooden gate along an ivy-lined path, passing two cottages, then bear right towards Kenwood House car park. (For a detour to the **Spaniards Inn** take the exit on to Spaniards Road and you'll find the inn 300yds (274m) on the left.)

④ To continue, bear right through the car park following signs to **Kenwood House**. Turn right, through the main gates. Take the path on the right of the house, through an ivy arch and on to a wide terrace that overlooks an expanse of grassland. Beyond the tea room take a left fork to a pergola, for fine views including Canary Wharf and the Post Office Tower. Next, take a path to the right, passing a metal gate.

⑤ Turn left, downhill, passing to the left of a lake. Keep ahead through some woodland and go through another metal gate.

Continue along the track ahead, take the next left fork and head uphill. At a fork take the left-hand path, which then descends. Follow the tarmac path past a pond.

⑥ Pass three more ponds to turn sharp right after the last one, along a path that climbs uphill. At the next junction follow the right-hand path to the top of **Parliament Hill**. Continue down this path, through the trees and between two ponds. Head uphill for 50yds (46m).

⑦ Turn left. After 250yds (229m) bear right on to a wider track, following it to **East Heath Road**. Cross over into **Devonshire Hill** and turn first left into **Keats Grove** to visit **Keats House**. Otherwise continue along Devonshire Hill, turning right at the end into **Rosslyn Hill**, then back up to **Hampstead tube**.

# Top Marx for Highgate

*Extend your walk to include Highgate and its celebrated cemetery.*
**See map and information panel for Walk 28**

| | |
|---|---|
| **•DISTANCE•** | 2 miles (3.2km) |
| **•MINIMUM TIME•** | 1hr |
| **•ASCENT / GRADIENT•** | 164ft (50m) |
| **•LEVEL OF DIFFICULTY•** | |

## Walk 29 Directions (Walk 28 option)

Leave the main route at Point ⑥. Turn right into **Millfield Lane**, right along **Highgate West Hill** and then left into **Swains Lane**, Point Ⓐ. Continue up this long hill to the twin entrances to **Highgate Cemetery**. In 1983 it was declared a place of outstanding historic and architectural interest – after just two minutes inside its 37 acres (15ha) you will understand why.

Built in 1839, the cemetery was one of seven private burial grounds completed during London's rapid expansion. Its 52,000 graves are marked by a mixture of memorials, gravestones, catacombs and mausoleums. Much of the upkeep is carried out by The Friends of Highgate Cemetery, who first began working here in 1975. They had a tough job as the cemetery had been neglected and was very overgrown. Now managed as a woodland, part of its charm lies in the randomness of its wild habitat.

Karl Marx is buried in the Eastern Cemetery, but you will need to join one of the remarkable tours to see the Western Cemetery. This is where the adventure really begins. Its Gothic architecture led John Betjeman to describe it as a 'Victorian Valhalla'.

Just past the cemetery, on the right, go through the gate leading into **Waterlow Park** (Point Ⓑ). This beautiful park was bequeathed to the people by Sydney Waterlow, as 'a garden for the gardenless'. Take the left fork and bear right through a row of trees. Cross the bridge and fork left (but not sharp left). At the top of the path, just after an aviary, turn left. Continue past a wall, to turn right, into the grounds of **Lauderdale House**. This was once a summer retreat of Charles II and his mistress, Nell Gwyn.

Continue past **Lauderdale House** and turn left into **Highgate High Street**. After 325yds (297m) turn left into **South Grove**, Point Ⓒ. A few paces further, on the left, is **St Michael's Church**, which has one of the most distinctive spires in north London. Samuel Taylor Coleridge is buried here and Dickens mentions the church in *David Copperfield*. Just as the road bends to the left past a white house, cross the road into **Merton Lane**. Continue along the path between two ponds, rejoining the main route at Point ⑥.

Walk 30

# The Seven Wonders of Kensington

*A simple route highlighting the architectural masterpieces in the museum district of west London.*

| | |
|---|---|
| •DISTANCE• | 2½ miles (4km) |
| •MINIMUM TIME• | 1hr |
| •ASCENT / GRADIENT• | Negligible |
| •LEVEL OF DIFFICULTY• | |
| •PATHS• | City pavements |
| •LANDSCAPE• | Busy city centre |
| •SUGGESTED MAP• | aqua3 OS Explorer 173 London North |
| •START• | Grid reference: TQ 269788; South Kensington tube |
| •FINISH• | Grid reference: TQ 254784; Earls Court tube |
| •DOG FRIENDLINESS• | Four-legged friends won't enjoy this one |
| •PUBLIC TOILETS• | None on route |

## Walk 30 Directions

This walk captures the spirit of the Great Exhibition of 1851, which was organised by Prince Albert, the Queen's Consort. The exhibition was so successful that it inspired him to establish a permanent centre for the study of the applied arts and sciences. He proposed that some of the profits from the exhibition should be used to buy land in South Kensington. The result was the world-class concentration of museums in South Kensington, and Imperial College. Although this is a relatively short walk you can easily spend a day here if you visit any of the museums.

### WHAT TO LOOK FOR ⓘ

The restoration of the **Albert Memorial** is one of English Heritage's most ambitious conservation projects to date. The memorial, which was stripped back to its cast-iron core and totally rebuilt, took four years to restore.

From **South Kensington tube** cross **Thurloe Street** and turn left into **Exhibition Road**. Cross the road at the traffic lights. On the right-hand corner is the **Victoria and Albert Museum**. On the opposite side of the road sits the splendid **Natural History Museum**. The walk continues along Exhibition Road past the **Science Museum,** on the left, followed by **Imperial College** (for science, technology and medicine). The Victoria and Albert Museum is regarded as one of the world's greatest museums. As it has more than 7 miles (11.3km) of galleries, it's hard to know where to begin. It's best to take your time and wander around slowly.

The neo-Gothic architecture of the Natural History Museum is extraordinary. Designed by Alfred Waterhouse, it uses the decorative terracotta that was so fashionable in the Victorian era to full effect. A series of lion sculptures also feature in the design. The Science Museum is less impressive outside – even some of its staff say that it resembles 'a small Selfridges'. In the early stages it was an odd collection of wooden buildings. The chief architect, Sir Richard Allison, had been asked to maintain the strictest economy in the new construction, which was built on a grand scale, as was the rambling hulk that is Imperial College.

---

**WHERE TO EAT AND DRINK** ⓘ

All the museums mentioned have either a café or restaurant. The **Victoria and Albert Museum's restaurant** serves wine and beers, and all dishes are made from fresh ingredients. The **Victoria Brasserie**, accessed from Door 2 of the Royal Albert Hall, has a buffet.

---

Turn left into **Prince Consort Road**, which is home to the 600 students of the Royal College of Music. If you see some oddly shaped rucksacks and bags, they probably belong to a musician or student at this school, which provides courses for performers and composers. In the concert hall sits an organ donated by the composer Hubert Parry, who taught here, as did Charles Villiers Stanford and Ralph Vaughan Williams.

Half-way along Prince Consort Road, on the right, there are some steps that lead up to the **Royal Albert Hall**, with its familiar red-domed roof. At the top of these bear right to reach the main road, **Kensington Gore**. Cross this at the traffic lights for a closer look at the **Albert Memorial**, only recently restored to its former glory in Kensington Gardens.

Retrace your steps back to the Royal Albert Hall. With the building on your left, continue along **Kensington Gore**, past the rather dull exterior of the Royal College of Art (in marked contrast to the decorative Estonian Embassy behind it), until you reach **Queen's Gate**. Turn left past the Gore Hotel and cross **Prince Consort Road**. On the left is the other end of Imperial College and soon you'll see the wildlife garden of the **Natural History Museum**, behind the railings where Queen's Gate meets Cromwell Road. Continue ahead, still on Queen's Gate, then take the first right into **Stanhope Gardens**, which then becomes **Harrington Gardens**. At the end of the road turn left, then soon right, into **Bramham Gardens**, to reach **Earls Court Road**. To visit the fascinating **West Brompton Cemetery**, turn left here, to Old Brompton Road, then go right. Otherwise turn right, to reach **Earls Court tube**.

---

**WHILE YOU'RE THERE** ⓘ

The **Earls Court Exhibition Centre** began life as a triangular-shaped, outdoor arena. It was the venue for the *Buffalo Bill Wild West Show*, an extravaganza that coincided with Queen Victoria's Golden Jubilee. The show included 100 North American Indians, most of who had never before ventured outside their native reservations. The show was so popular that the Queen requested a performance at Windsor Castle before it went on tour to Europe. One reviewer at the time wrote 'It is new, it is brilliant, it is startling, it will go!' The present building opened in 1937 and was designed by the Detroit architect C Howard Crabem, who had made his name designing theatres all over North America. In nearby **West Brompton Cemetery** are the graves of two of the North American Indians who died in Britain after coming over to perform in the *Buffalo Bill Wild West Show*. One was Chief Long Wolf who died at the age of 59.

# Roses and Romance Around Regent's Park

*Rose gardens, an open-air theatre, panoramic views from Primrose Hill, birdsong along the Regent's Canal, and Little Venice.*

| | |
|---|---|
| •DISTANCE• | 3¼ miles (5.3km) |
| •MINIMUM TIME• | 1hr 30min |
| •ASCENT / GRADIENT• | 131ft (40m) ▲ ▲ ▲ |
| •LEVEL OF DIFFICULTY• | 🚶 🚶 🚶 |
| •PATHS• | Paved streets and tarmac paths |
| •LANDSCAPE• | Exclusive properties and idyllic park |
| •SUGGESTED MAP• | AA Street by Street London |
| •START• | Baker Street tube |
| •FINISH• | Warwick Avenue tube |
| •DOG FRIENDLINESS• | No particular problems |
| •PUBLIC TOILETS• | None on route |

## BACKGROUND TO THE WALK

> *'I must go seek some dew-drops here*
> *And hang a pearl in every cowslip's ear'*

So sings the Fairy to Puck in *A Midsummer Night's Dream*, William Shakespeare's romantic fantasy. If you think that romance is dead, you need to try this walk, especially on weekdays, when it's quieter. Along these canals you'll see barges rather than gondolas, but on a fine, balmy day you can return to Regent's Park in the evening to see a performance at the magical open-air theatre, and there isn't one of those in Venice. You never know, this walk could well turn out to be a recurring midsummer night's dream.

### Nash's Dream

'It shall be called Bottom's Dream because it hath no bottom…' wrote Shakespeare. In a similar way, this walk was John Nash's dream because, in 1820 when he designed the area, it was the grandest piece of town planning ever devised in central London. In fact, it has not been matched since. His scheme was based on a park peppered with large villas that looked like separate mansions but which actually consisted of more than 20 houses. Sprinkle on to this some grand terraces and the result is idyllic Regent's Park and its little sister, Primrose Hill. Although only 210ft (64m) above sea level, the views over London from Primrose Hill are exhilarating.

### A Pucker Venue

If you're lucky enough to find that *A Midsummer Night's Dream* is on at the open-air theatre, don't expect it to be one of Shakespeare's best stories, for it's about ideas rather than plot. 'The course of true love never runs smooth' explained the bard and this concept carries on throughout the play. Shakespeare uses the common theme of a daughter who wants to marry against her father's wishes and the comic caricatures are portrayed by Bottom and

Puck. Since the play was first published in 1600 it has been the source of inspiration for countless stories of tiny fairies living in the woods. Walt Disney made a fortune from the idea, but it didn't entertain the prominent diarist Samuel Pepys, who saw it in 1662 for the first time and wrote: '... nor shall I ever (see it) again, for it is the most insipid ridiculous play that I ever saw in my life'. Pepys did, however, admit to appreciating the play's good dancing and attractive women!

Had Pepys seen it in the unique setting of Regent's Park however he might have thought differently. He could have arrived early to picnic and drink champagne on the lawn, and afterwards taken a stroll to Primrose Hill to see London's carpet of flickering lights below. Try it one midsummer's day and if this little potion doesn't bring some magic into your life, you'll have to ask Puck for some help.

**Walk 31**

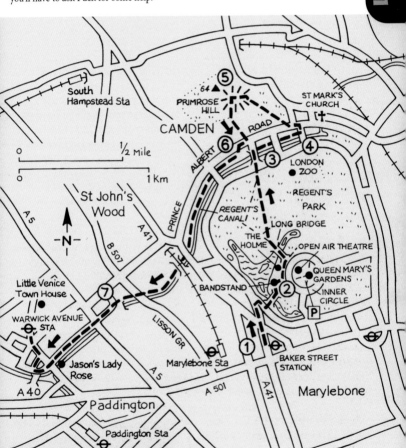

# Walk 31 Directions

① Take the north exit from **Baker Street tube** and turn right, along **Baker Street**. Cross the road via two sets of pedestrian lights and enter **Regent's Park**. Turn right. Cross the bridge over the lake and then bear left, past the bandstand.

② Turn left when you reach the Inner Circle road. Beyond **The Holme** turn left, through the metal gates, and over **Long Bridge**. When the paths fork ahead, take the right-hand one and keep ahead at the next crossing of paths.

③ Go through the gate, cross the Outer Circle road and follow the path opposite to cross **Primrose Hill Bridge**. Turn left along a path leading down to the **Regent's Canal**, then turn sharp left. Continue along this path – which initially leads underneath the bridge and then leads past the aviary of London Zoo – for ¼ mile (400m). You'll also pass under a couple of bridges with ornate ironwork and some colourful canal boats.

> **WHILE YOU'RE THERE** ⓘ
> Take a wander through the circular **Queen Mary's Gardens** inside the Inner Circle of Regent's Park. You can reach them by taking the path ahead instead of turning left after the bandstand. Enclosed by hedges, the rose gardens are quiet, yet vibrant and include a fountain.

④ At the second bridge turn left up the path leading to **St Mark's Church**. At the gate turn left along **Prince Albert Road** and past an entrance to London Zoo. Continue for 100yds (91m) then, at the pedestrian lights, cross the road to enter **Primrose Hill**. Take the right-hand path and follow it uphill to the viewpoint.

⑤ Follow the path that bears left, leading downhill, to join a straight path that leads to **Prince Albert Road**. Cross at the zebra crossing and turn right. At a footpath, signed 'Canalside Walk', turn left.

⑥ Don't cross the bridge but turn right along a hedge-lined path that bends sharply to the left on to the tow path. Turn right and follow the

> **WHERE TO EAT AND DRINK** ⓘ
> Just a few paces from Warwick Avenue tube lies the **Little Venice Town House** in Warrington Crescent. The building was once a hospital (it has an unusually shaped lift that carried stretchers to the old operating theatre) and it was here that Alan Turing, the mathematician responsible for breaking the Enigma code during the Second World War, was born in 1912. Pop in here for afternoon tea after the walk. Alternatively, **Jason's** *Lady Rose* canal boat has outdoor seating adjacent to the canal in Little Venice.

tow path for ½ mile (800m). The banks of the canal are ivy-clad with weeping willows, and palatial homes line this stretch of the walk. Continue ahead under the railway bridges – less enchanting but rest assured that better things lie ahead – and, after a few paces, you'll pass the houseboats moored at **Lisson Green** before a tow path tunnel.

⑦ As the canal disappears under another tunnel, walk up the steps on the right and continue ahead along **Aberdeen Place**. At the end cross a road and follow **Blomfield Road** into **Little Venice**. Cross **Warwick Avenue** and follow the road as it bends to the right, past the footbridge. Turn right into **Warwick Place** and then left again to find **Warwick Avenue tube** 100yds (91m) ahead.

> **WHAT TO LOOK FOR** ⓘ
> **Regent's Park's Open Air Theatre** was founded in 1932 and is the premier professional outdoor theatre in Great Britain. Many well-known artists have appeared here during the summer season including Deborah Kerr, Vivian Leigh, Felicity Kendal, Jeremy Irons and Maria Aitken. With seating for well over 1,000, it's larger than the Barbican and the Olivier Theatre on the South Bank.

# Big Screen Diversions in Holland Park

*Holland Park has something for everyone: cinemas, cafés, wildlife and memorable architecture.*

| | |
|---|---|
| •DISTANCE• | 3¼ miles (5.3km) |
| •MINIMUM TIME• | 1hr 30min |
| •ASCENT / GRADIENT• | 66ft (20m) ▲ ▲ ▲ |
| •LEVEL OF DIFFICULTY• | 🚶🚶 🚶🚶 🚶 |
| •PATHS• | Paved streets and tarmac paths |
| •LANDSCAPE• | Exclusive properties and an idyllic park |
| •SUGGESTED MAP• | AA Street by Street London |
| •START / FINISH• | Notting Hill Gate tube |
| •DOG FRIENDLINESS• | On lead near peacocks and in woodland areas |
| •PUBLIC TOILETS• | Holland Park and Notting Hill Gate |

## BACKGROUND TO THE WALK

The walk begins at Notting Hill Gate, for it wouldn't be fair to mention 'diversions' without including Holland Park's lively neighbour, Notting Hill. Most cinema audiences throughout the world are now familiar with this area thanks to the film of the same name, starring Julia Roberts and Hugh Grant. The blue front door that featured in many scenes was, at that time, the home of Richard Curtis, the film's scriptwriter. And of course, there's that colourful annual event known as the Notting Hill Carnival that takes place in August, not to mention the world-famous Portobello Road antiques market… but where does Holland Park fit into all this?

### The Tortoise

Holland Park is a bit like Aesop's fable about the tortoise and the hare. While it may lack the racy pace of its neighbour, it knows its limitations and is comfortable in its own, refined skin. Some of the architecture here is truly memorable. The area includes some of the most sought-after properties in London but it has a soft centre in the form of a delightful 54 acre (22ha) park, in which lie the partial ruins of a Jacobean mansion, Holland House.

Lady Holland hosted some lavish parties in this building for guests including Lord Byron, Earl Grey, Lord Palmerston and Charles Dickens. The building was largely destroyed during the Blitz in the Second World War. The section that remains is now a youth hostel with 201 beds. For less than the cost of a theatre ticket you can stay overnight in one of the loveliest parks in London. You can still see some remnants from the house's glorious past, such as the old ballroom (which is now a Marco Pierre White restaurant called The Belvedere) and the manicured garden that includes a mural of an 1870s garden party.

### Smokers' Zone

And that's not all. Take the striking Gate Cinema, for example: it was was once a theatre and now shows international films. If it's open you should take a peek inside, as you should with the Coronet, a little further on. The Coronet is now the only cinema in London to permit smoking during the film, although non-smokers usually find safety in the stalls, as smokers are restricted to the dress circle. Addison Road also has its fair share of architectural delights. Keep an eye out for No 8, a monster of a house that was designed for the store magnate, Sir Ernest Debenham. Love it or hate it, this building is so 'in your face' that it's hard not to form an immediate opinion of the turquoise and blue glazed brickwork.

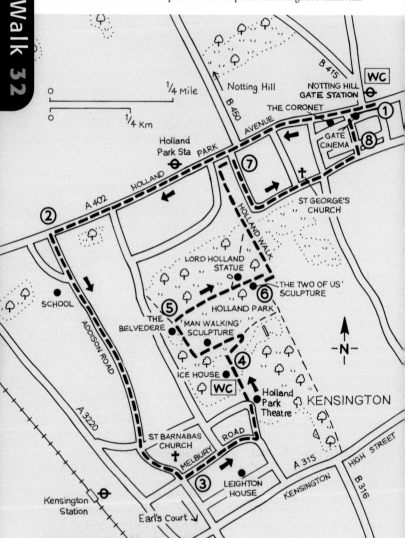

## Walk 32 Directions

① From **Notting Hill Gate tube** head towards **Holland Park Avenue**, passing the **Gate Cinema** and a few paces further, the

**Coronet**. This busy road is lined with some quaint shops and pubs, including one of the finest organic butchers in London.

② About 650yds (594m) after **Holland Park tube** turn left into

**Walk 32**

**Holland Park Gardens**. Just after the red brick school on the right the road joins **Addison Road**.

③ Turn left past St Barnabas Church into **Melbury Road**. Cross **Abbotsbury Road** and continue to the next road. Look out for the huge palm trees in the manicured garden on the corner. Turn left here to reach the gates of **Holland Park**. Take the path ahead and walk through the arch. On the left is the ice house.

④ Bear right through the hedged garden and, after passing under another arch, turn left to follow the footpath as it descends a set of stone steps. The strange man you see with rolled-up sleeves walking towards you is, in fact, a realistic bronze sculpture. Follow the path as it swings to the right.

⑤ At the end of this fenced path turn right along a long, straight path that heads slightly uphill, flanked by lime trees. Ahead is a statue of Lord Holland sitting high above a pond, the local watering hole for squirrels. If you're a keen birdwatcher, take a look in the woods behind the pond. Otherwise continue towards another sculpture.

⑥ Make what you will of this huge bronze entitled *The Two of Us* by contemporary sculptor Stephen Gregory, then turn right. Soon go left and pass a metal gate. Turn left along **Holland Walk**, a tarmac path also used by cyclists (if you turn right here you'll end up on Kensington High Street). Follow Holland Walk to the end.

⑦ Turn right and take the next right, **Aubrey Road**, which has an eclectic mix of architectural styles. Follow it as it bends to the left and later passes **St George's Church**. At the crossroads continue ahead, turning into the first road on the left, **Hillgate Street**.

⑧ After crossing **Hillgate Place** and its attractive rows of pastel-coloured terraced houses, turn right into **Notting Hill Gate** and back to the start.

Walk 33

# An Aromatic Oasis in Morden

*A short but lingering walk through the fragrant gardens of Morden Hall Park in suburban south London.*

| | |
|---|---|
| •DISTANCE• | 1¾ miles (2.8km) |
| •MINIMUM TIME• | 1hr |
| •ASCENT / GRADIENT• | Negligible |
| •LEVEL OF DIFFICULTY• | |
| •PATHS• | Mainly tarmac paths |
| •LANDSCAPE• | Parkland, marshland and meadows |
| •SUGGESTED MAP• | aqua3 OS Explorer 161 London South |
| •START / FINISH• | Grid reference: TQ 257686; Morden tube |
| •DOG FRIENDLINESS• | Remember to poop-scoop in Morden Hall Park |
| •PARKING• | At garden centre off Morden Hall Road (Morden tube 550yds/500m) |
| •PUBLIC TOILETS• | Morden Hall Park |

## BACKGROUND TO THE WALK

Morden Hall Park is fittingly described in the National Trust Handbook as 'a green oasis in the heart of London suburbia'. If it's your first visit here then you cannot fail to be impressed by the array of old estate buildings and ancient hay meadows. If you are a budding gardener, you'll relish the sight and scent of the rose garden in summer but if history is your thing, you can discover more about Morden's snuff-milling industry.

### A Garden of Roses

The rose garden is worthy of a mention because recent restoration by the National Trust returned it to its former glory. With names like *Golden Wedding*, *Harvest Fair*, *Iceberg* and *English Miss* you can probably guess the colours. The 2 acre (0.8ha) rose garden was originally created in 1921. Unlike most gardens of this kind, the 48 rose beds are randomly laid out, rather than in a symmetrical pattern. The beds are shaped like horseshoes, crescents and half-moons and they are seen best from the eastern side of the garden. Because there were no records of the original plants used, modern floribunda roses were chosen to produce the vivid abundance of colour, which reaches its peak in June.

### Not to be Sniffed At

Morden Hall Park belonged to the Hatfeild family, which made its money from snuff milling. The family formed a firm of tobacconists, Taddy, Tomlin and Hatfeild of Fenchurch Street, in the City of London. You can see the remains of their snuff mill, powered by the River Wandle, in the park. Snuff was ground by hand until water-powered mills took over in the 18th century. These operated on a pestle and mortar principle, crushing the tobacco leaves to a fine powder. It was a dusty environment and workers used sponge respirators to help them breathe. Demand for snuff was high during the 1800s – and these mills were just two of hundreds throughout the country.

### Morden Hall Revisited

Morden Hall Park was once self-sufficient. It had a deer park (venison), grazing meadows (milk) and kitchen gardens (fresh fruit and vegetables). When the bachelor Gilliat Hatfeild died in 1941, he left the bulk of his 125 acre (51ha) estate to the National Trust, with a clause in his will stating that the park should be open to the public. Hatfeild was a conservative man, refusing gas or electricity, and had no interest in buying the latest form of transport, the motor car. He was also a kind employer, providing the staff with food at Christmas and inviting the local children to parties in the grounds. Today, Morden Hall Park is a remarkable reminder of this bygone era.

## Walk 33 Directions

① Turn left at the exit to **Morden tube**. At the junction use the pedestrian crossing to cross **Morden Road**. Bear right along **Morden Hall Road**. Ignore the first entrance on the left leading to

**Morden Hall** (now occupied by a chain pub/restaurant outlet), and take the second. Follow the path ahead, past the stable block on your right, leading to the tea room and garden centre.

② Cross the bridge, passing the **Snuff Mill Environmental Centre** (primarily an educational facility for school groups), to enter the lower section of the rose garden. You can walk across the grass but you need to return across the bridge and turn right.

③ A few paces further, turn right over a white bridge with decorative iron railings and walk along an avenue of lime and chestnut trees to cross a bridge over a tributary of the River Wandle.

> **WHAT TO LOOK FOR** ⓘ
> On either side of the rose garden's path you will see Robina pseud acacia (**False Acacia**). This tree is named after Jean Robin, a French botanist but it didn't become popular until William Cobbett sold over one million trees after returning from America in the early 1800s. False Acacia produces a pea-shaped, fragrant, white blossom similar to the laburnum, and its timber makes good gate- and fence-posts.

④ Turn right and go through a metal gate leading to the upper section of the rose garden. Follow the path ahead to reach another metal gate. Continue past the pond, with its wilderness islands, as it curves to the left to meet the avenue of lime and chestnut trees.

⑤ Follow the path as it swings to the left, becoming a narrow path beside some fencing. A few paces

> **WHERE TO EAT AND DRINK** ⓘ
> The **National Trust tea rooms** by the shop are a good option, as is **Morden Hall**, part of Whitbreads' Out and Out chain, which has restaurants, bars and gardens, although not much remains of the original building. Overlooking the River Wandle (on Walk 34) you'll find the **William Morris** pub, which has a sun terrace; this free house serves a range of award-winning beers and real ales.

further on, when the path joins another, take the left-hand fork across the meadow.

⑥ Just before the road and tram stop, turn diagonally left across the meadow towards the avenue of trees. At the main path turn right and retrace your steps from Point ④ towards the white bridge, and then back to **Morden tube**.

> **WHILE YOU'RE THERE** ⓘ
> Pay a visit to the **craft workshops** and **information room** beside the tea room to discover more about the hall and its park. The older of the two mills ground snuff from the mid-1750s right up until 1922. While we may have Sir Walter Raleigh to thank for introducing pipe smoking from North America, Spanish conquistadors discovered the habit of inhaling snuff through the nose in South America. It wasn't without controversy, for a person caught taking snuff in the mid-1600s was under threat of having his nose amputated! During snuff's heyday – the Regency period – a man was judged by his ornate snuff box and quality of the blend it contained. Today, there are still more than 300 blends of snuff available.

# On to Merton Abbey Mills

*Follow the Wandle Trail to the site of William Morris' print works.*
**See map and information panel for Walk 33**

| | |
|---|---|
| •DISTANCE• | 3 miles (4.8km) |
| •MINIMUM TIME• | 2hrs |
| •ASCENT / GRADIENT• | Negligible |
| •LEVEL OF DIFFICULTY• | |

## Walk 34 Directions (Walk 33 option)

To complete a linear walk to Collier's Wood tube, leave the main route at the white bridge, Point ③. Turn right over two more footbridges and then fork right to cross a third bridge. The views across the first two bridges are delightful – notice the moat and the remains of decorative brick bridges draped in ivy. The path later cuts through the wetland area, much favoured by birdwatchers, before reaching a wooden gate, Point Ⓐ.

Turn right, signposted 'Deen City Farm' and 'Phipps Bridge', along an enclosed path. Cross the level crossing and turn right over a little bridge that spans a ditch. Follow the track around the edge of **Bunce's Meadow** and past **Deen City Farm**, Point Ⓑ. Continue ahead for 200yds (183m) and cross **Windsor Avenue**. About 300yds (274m) further, just before the next road, turn right to reach the entrance to **Merton Abbey Mills**, Point Ⓒ. The Wheel House here is a Grade II listed building. It once drove machinery in Liberty's print works. After exploring the craft shops, cafés and the **William Morris** pub,

retrace your steps to the **River Wandle** where, instead of turning right, continue ahead to cross **Merantum Way** at the pedestrian lights. Pass through a brick arch and rejoin the riverside **Wandle Trail**. Follow this to a footbridge beside a superstore.

Just before the Sava-Centre footbridge is an apartment block. It stands on the site of William Morris's Merton Abbey Print Works. Morris was born in 1834 and he is best remembered for his textile and wallpaper designs. His approach to arts and crafts was: 'honest, original work… properly rewarded, not sweated'. His company, Morris & Co, produced stained glass, textiles and dyed silk and created over 40 chintz patterns. One of these, the Wandle chintz, was so named 'to honour our helpful stream'. Concerned with the preservation of buildings, Morris was a pioneer of the environmental movement, so it's a sad irony that no trace of his print works remains today.

Turn left, over the footbridge, on to **Merton High Street**. Bear right and follow the road that crosses a bridge. Cross the junction over two sets of pedestrian lights to reach **Collier's Wood tube**, Point Ⓓ.

**Walk 35**

# Secrets of the Natural Wimbledon Common

*A nature walk around the famous Wimbledon Common, now protected as a Site of Special Scientific Interest.*

| | |
|---|---|
| •DISTANCE• | 2¾ miles (4.4km) |
| •MINIMUM TIME• | 1hr 30min |
| •ASCENT / GRADIENT• | 98ft (30m) ▲ ▲▲ ▲ |
| •LEVEL OF DIFFICULTY• | 👫 👫 👫 |
| •PATHS• | Gravel, tarmac and woodland paths |
| •LANDSCAPE• | Open heath and woodland |
| •SUGGESTED MAP• | aqua3 OS Explorer 161 London South |
| •START / FINISH• | Grid reference: TQ 229726; Wimbledon rail 1½ miles (2.4km) |
| •DOG FRIENDLINESS• | No particular problems |
| •PARKING• | Car park by Wimbledon Common Windmill |
| •PUBLIC TOILETS• | At car park |

## Walk 35 Directions

If you are unfamiliar with this area, you may be surprised to discover that 495 acres (200ha) of Wimbledon Common comprises thick woodland, with the rest made up of heath and grassland. In 1987 the Common was designated a Site of Special Scientific Interest (SSSI) as its proximity to London makes its valley mires unique. While heathland in other areas has fallen prey to developments such as

---

**WHERE TO EAT AND DRINK** ℹ️
**Wimbledon Tearooms**, by the Windmill car park, has seating inside and out and prides itself on its freshly-cooked food. Snacks include toasted sandwiches and jacket potatoes and an interesting array of baguette fillings. Hot meals include a mixed grill. If you're after sofas and a brasserie-style restaurant, the **Common Room** in nearby Wimbledon village serves light, healthy dishes.

---

supermarkets and airports, Wimbledon Common's status as a candidate for a Special Area of Conservation (SAC) has ensured its protection from such an outcome.

From the car park walk back along the road to a junction. Turn right here and pass beside a metal gate. Ignore the path on the left after about 300yds (274m) and continue ahead alongside a bridleway. After the next junction the path curves to the right and crosses the **Royal Wimbledon Golf Course** (beware of low-flying golf balls). At a fork, follow the left-hand track to a tarmac road. Cross it and take the path opposite, across the heath towards the trees – follow the track through this woodland area.

By the 1860s, Wimbledon Common had come in to the ownership of Earl Spencer, as titular Lord of the Manor of Wimbledon. In 1864 he revealed plans to enclose 700 acres

Walk 35

(289ha) of common for parkland, a garden and house building. Though the commoners raised few objections, the Enclosure Bill stalled in the committee stage as MPs had become increasingly concerned about London's diminishing open spaces. After seven years of legal wrangling, a solution was found in the Wimbledon and Putney Commons Act of 1871. Earl Spencer was compensated for his lost land, and the rights of the common were passed to conservators, charged with preserving their natural character. Between them, Putney Heath and Wimbledon Common now contain 50 per cent of London's heathland. But these are not the only natural credentials about which the commons can boast. This is also a prime site for the endangered stag beetle.

At a T-junction turn right, downhill. Continue through the woods with the golf course on your left. Take a right-hand fork (the left one hugs the perimeter of the golf course) and then pass through three concrete posts, leading to a path on the right. The next stretch of the walk, which later curves right again, passes some buildings and continues for about a mile (1.6km).

Cross a brook at a junction and continue to another fork. Ignore the small path to the right and take the

> ### WHILE YOU'RE THERE
> The **interpretation centre** in the rangers' office, on the other side of the tea rooms, illustrates how the Common is maintained, what the role of a ranger involves and explains how the wildlife can be managed. There are some wildlife exhibits and also facilities for group lectures. During the mushroom season (mid-September to late November) you can join one of the organised Fungi Forays, to discover more about the fascinating underground route network of mushrooms. The 'fruiting head' that you see above ground is only the tip of this intriguing woodland iceberg.

next right fork, which in turn swings to the right and runs parallel to some playing fields. Keep on this gentle, uphill track through woodland, but stop to take a look at the war memorial beyond the playing fields. Continue past some buildings on your left and 100yds (91m) further on, a cemetery in **Putney Vale**. The path descends gradually. On the right, opposite a metal gate to the cemetery, look out for a red brick ditch. Turn right over this ditch until the path opens up to **Queen's Mere**, a picturesque pond much favoured by dogs.

Follow the path with Queen's Mere on your right. At the end take the track uphill, bearing right. At the top turn left and walk back to the car park.

> ### WHAT TO LOOK FOR
> Each year on Wimbledon Common the park ranger team identifies at least 200 species of **mushroom**, of which only 10 per cent are inedible, have no culinary value or are poisonous. The mushrooms extract foods from decaying matter, which is nature's way of recycling, and so mushrooms here should not be picked. Many of them attract a lot of attention, especially the Wood blewit and the Boletus species, which are highly prized on the Continent. Although grey squirrels are abundant and foxes are often seen, some less obvious (in fact, very elusive) creatures sharing the Common are the bank vole, the short-tailed vole, the pygmy shrew, grass snakes and the occasional stoat. The woodlands also support five species of bat.

# With the Wetland Birds of Barnes

*Explore the award-winning London Wetland Centre and join the course of the Oxford and Cambridge Boat Race.*

| | |
|---|---|
| •DISTANCE• | 3¾ miles (6km) |
| •MINIMUM TIME• | 1hr 30min |
| •ASCENT / GRADIENT• | Negligible |
| •LEVEL OF DIFFICULTY• | |
| •PATHS• | Riverside tow path, muddy after rain |
| •LANDSCAPE• | Views across Thames |
| •SUGGESTED MAP• | aqua3 OS Explorer 161 London South |
| •START / FINISH• | Grid reference: TQ 227767; Barnes Bridge rail ¾ mile (1.2km) or bus 283 (known as 'the Duck Bus') from Hammersmith tube |
| •DOG FRIENDLINESS• | London Wetland Centre (LWC) is no-go area for dogs |
| •PARKING• | At LWC (pay if not visiting) |
| •PUBLIC TOILETS• | At London Wetland Centre |

## BACKGROUND TO THE WALK

Rowing boats, like birds, glide gracefully through water and also, like birds, you'll see plenty of them during this easy walk. Barnes has long been associated with the Oxford and Cambridge Boat Race. Indeed, the footbridge, added in 1895, was specifically designed to hold the crowds watching the last stage of the 4⅓ mile (7km) race to Mortlake.

### Loads of Birds
The riverside functions rather like a wildlife highway, providing a natural habitat for birds. There are plenty of them to see without having to put a foot inside the London Wetland Centre (LWC) – but to omit it would be to miss out on a very rewarding experience. So why not extend the walk and visit the LWC? There are more than 2 miles (3.2km) of paths and 650yds (594m) of boardwalk to explore once you have paid the admission charge.

### Four Reservoirs and a Vision
The mother hen of all bird sanctuaries is the Wildfowl and Wetlands Trust at Slimbridge in Gloucestershire. It was founded by Sir Peter Scott, son of the great explorer, Scott of the Antarctic. One of his father's diaries carries the words: 'teach the boy nature' and this was indeed achieved, for Peter Scott became a renowned painter and naturalist. In recognition of his achievements, a larger-than-life sculpture of him stands on a raised gravel island at the entrance to the LWC, the only inner city wetland reserve in the world.

There are now nine wetland centres in the UK. This one began with four redundant reservoirs owned by Thames Water. They formed a partnership with the housing developer, Berkeley Homes and donated £11 million to help construct the centre. The 105 acre (43ha) project took five years to complete. In 2001 the centre won the British Airways *Tourism for Tomorrow* award.

Once inside, there are three main sections: world wetlands, reserve habitats and waterlife. The first contains captive birds from around the world – North America is accessed via a log cabin complete with authentic furniture. There are information panels too. One of them contradicts the popular belief that swans mate for life. Another tells us about meadowsweet, which is found in damp woods and marshes and used in herbal teas, mead flavouring and even air fresheners.

### A Chorus of Facts

Back to birds, and why do they make so much noise? The dawn chorus is their way of telling other birds where they are – 'keep off my patch!' is the message – but it's also to attract a mate. Some birds with colourful plumage find this easy, but others have developed a distinctive song to attract attention, of which the cuckoo is a good example.

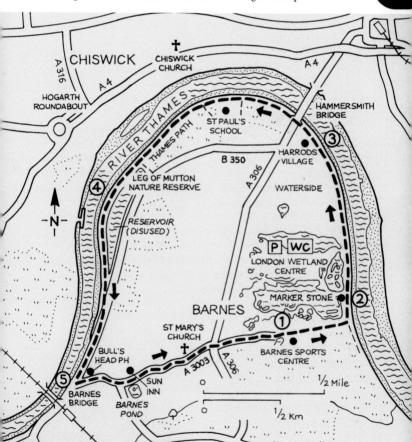

## Walk 36 Directions

① Turn left out of the **London Wetland Centre** and follow the path, initially to the left of the **Barnes Sports Centre** and then beside some sports fields. At a T-junction turn left along the well-signposted **Thames Path**, alongside the river in the direction of Hammersmith Bridge.

② About 100yds (91m) along the path on the left is a stone post, denoting the 1 mile (1.6km) marker of the Oxford and Cambridge University Boat Race. Steve Fairbairn, who was born in 1862, founded the Head of the River Race and this was the start of the world-famous, annual boat race that traditionally takes place in March.

> ### WHILE YOU'RE THERE ⓘ
> Chiswick church could once be reached by a ferry across the Thames, but since 1934 the only way is by bridge. The artist William Hogarth (from whom the Hogarth Roundabout takes its name) is buried in the churchyard. At the rear of the Sun Inn is **Barnes Bowling Club**, where Sir Francis Drake is said to have taught Elizabeth I the game of bowls.

③ The landscaped area of smart flats on the left is called **Waterside** and, a few paces further, a red brick building bears the name Harrods Village. Once past this, as if replicating the trademark Harrods colours of green and gold, is **Hammersmith Bridge**. Follow the path past **St Paul's School**, where *Planets* composer Gustav Holst was a music teacher. On the opposite side of the river, Chiswick Church's green roof is visible.

④ Turn left through a wooden gate into the **Leg of Mutton Nature Reserve**. Continue along the path to the right of this stretch of water, which was once a reservoir. When

> ### WHAT TO LOOK FOR ⓘ
> The development, **Waterside**, was constructed by Berkeley Homes after the company purchased 25 acres (10ha) and built the luxury homes that have a unique, bird's eye view of the centre and its wildlife. Adjacent, the **Harrods Village** building was once used to store furniture by those taking up posts in the British Empire. Derelict, it was also sold to Berkeley Homes and it now contains 250 flats with green window frames. Even the security guard wears a Harrods green and gold uniform.

the path swerves to the left, leave by a wooden gate to the right. Turn left and follow the riverside path towards **Barnes Bridge**.

⑤ Just past the **Bull's Head** pub turn left into **Barnes High Road**. At the next junction, by the little pond, bear left into **Church Road**. Past the **Sun Inn** is a row of village shops and 100yds (91m) further on, the lychgate to **St Mary's Church**. At the traffic lights continue ahead to return to the **London Wetland Centre** and the start of the walk.

> ### WHERE TO EAT AND DRINK ⓘ
> Unlike many on-site cafés, the **Water's Edge Café** at the London Wetland Centre is a delight. It's bright and spacious, serves good quality soups, sandwiches, salads and cakes, and has outdoor seating on large, wooden tables with umbrellas. There are also newspapers to read. The south-facing **Sun Inn** on Church Road, opposite Barnes duck pond lives up to its name – it's quite a suntrap in summer. The usual home-cooked food with a choice of vegetarian options is available here, as is a selection of Tetley's ales and Fuller's London Pride, which is brewed in nearby Chiswick.

# Along the Thames to the Gardens at Kew

*View the famous Royal Botanic Gardens at Kew from a surprisingly peaceful stretch of the Thames Path.*

Walk 37

| | |
|---|---|
| •DISTANCE• | 7½ miles (12.1km) |
| •MINIMUM TIME• | 3hrs |
| •ASCENT / GRADIENT• | Negligible |
| •LEVEL OF DIFFICULTY• | |
| •PATHS• | Mainly tow paths and tarmac |
| •LANDSCAPE• | Riverside gardens and pubs |
| •SUGGESTED MAP• | aqua3 OS Explorer 161 London South |
| •START / FINISH• | Grid reference: TQ 192767; Kew Gardens tube |
| •DOG FRIENDLINESS• | No problems (guide dogs only inside Kew Gardens) |
| •PUBLIC TOILETS• | Syon House |

## BACKGROUND TO THE WALK

Kew Gardens began life as a royal front lawn for Kew Palace, where George III lived during his years of mental illness. The collection of exotic plants here was started in the 1740s. Nearly a century later, in 1841, Queen Victoria handed the 300 acre (122ha) site to the nation as a public research institute. Since then it has grown from strength to strength, and is now the world's leading botanical research centre. Although this walk allows a glimpse along its boundaries, a visit inside is highly recommended, for which you should allow a few extra hours.

### Green Fingers

With the largest, living plant collection in the world, you'd expect there to be a lot of green fingers at Kew Gardens and there are. In fact 200 horticultural staff are responsible for mowing the lawns, looking after the tropical plants in the glasshouses and the Herbarium, where more than 6 million specimens of dried plants and fungi are stored. There are a further 100 scientists studying the medicinal importance of plants and many others based at one of the most visited parts of Kew, the Palm House.

### From the Outside Looking In

Depending on the time of the year, you may be able to see part of the Rhododendron Dell from the Thames Path. The river provides these spectacular shrubs with the humidity they love and although the soil is not naturally favourable, it has been treated with high-acidity mulch and sulphur to reduce the pH level. Rhododendrons are native to the Himalayas and were introduced to this country by the intrepid Victorians in the 1850s. There are now over 700 specimens of hardy species and hybrids in this Dell, some of which are unique to Kew Gardens. Flowering can extend from November to August but the best time to see the vivid array is late May.

Further along the Thames Path is the Syon Vista, an opening that affords views of the long, straight avenue leading to the Palm House. In keeping with the Victorian love of all things iron, the entire structure was built of iron and filled in with curved glass. However, in the mid 1980s it was deemed necessary to conduct some major restoration work and all the plants were removed and taken to a temporary home. It was not an easy task and the oldest pot plant in the world, the Encephalartos altensteinii, was enclosed in a special scaffold to avoid damage.

The Palm House contains a tropical rainforest where plants are divided into three sections: African, American, and Asia and the Pacific. A central area displays the tallest palm trees. If you decide to visit, you'll see not only some rare tropical plants but also ones that are now actually extinct elsewhere.

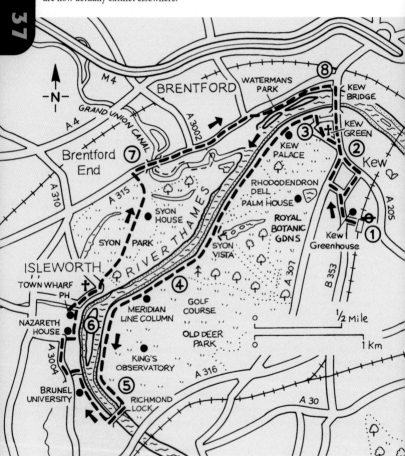

# Walk 37 Directions

① From the tube, follow the road ahead past the row of shops and turn right along **Sandycombe Road**, which becomes **Kew Gardens Road** as it bends to the left. At the main road opposite the **Royal Botanic Gardens**, turn right and continue ahead to the traffic lights. Cross **Kew Green** and head towards the church on the green.

② Take the path to the left of **St Anne's Church**, which was built for Queen Anne in 1714, and with your back to the church columns

### WHILE YOU'RE THERE   ⓘ
The beautiful **Great Conservatory** in Syon Park was built in 1820 for the 3rd Duke of Northumberland by the designer of Covent Garden Market, Charles Fowler. The present Duke of Northumberland still owns Syon House but prefers to stay at Alnwick Castle in Northumberland, which is where the broomstick sequences were filmed in the first Harry Potter movie.

follow the main path to the right. Once across the green, continue along **Ferry Lane** which leads to the **Thames Path**.

③ Turn left here following the river along an attractive stretch of the path that borders **Kew Gardens** and offers the outsider a tempting view of the famous botanic gardens from the other side of a formidable ivy-clad walled ditch.

④ Just after a field, cross a ditch with metal gates to the left, signifying that this is the boundary of the **Old Deer Park**, which is now the home of the Royal Mid-Surrey Golf Course. Continue walking ahead for a further mile (1.6km) on the obvious track and cross **Richmond Lock** to reach the other side of the Thames.

⑤ Follow the riverside path past a boatyard where the **Capital Ring path** veers away from the river to run by the **Twickenham Campus** of Brunel University. When you reach the road turn right and just past the convent, **Nazareth House**, turn right at a mini-roundabout, signposted 'Thames Path'.

⑥ Turn left alongside the river towards the popular chalet-style **Town Wharf** pub and here, bear left and turn first right into

**Church Street**. Go over a bridge, past the riverside **London Apprentice** pub. After a church the road swings to the left along **Park Road**. Enter **Syon Park** and follow the wide, tarmac road.

⑦ Exit the park via a walled path and turn right at the road. Cross a bridge and, if this path isn't flooded, turn right for a detour along the **Grand Union Canal**. Otherwise continue along the road ahead bearing right to go through **Watermans Park** and then rejoining the **Thames Path**.

### WHAT TO LOOK FOR   ⓘ
About 440yds (400m) past the ditch marking the boundary of the Old Deer Park, you'll come to a silver column showing the **Meridian Line**. The vista across to the King's Observatory includes the original Meridian Line that was used to set the King's time at the Houses of Parliament before 1884 when the Greenwich Meridian Line became the standard, (▶ Background to Walk 8).

⑧ Past an ever-present row of houseboats, turn right to cross **Kew Bridge**. Cross the road at a pedestrian crossing, continue ahead and bear left into **Mortlake Road**. Turn right into **Cumberland Road** and left at the end to retrace your steps along **Kew Gardens Road** back to the tube station at the start of the walk.

### WHERE TO EAT AND DRINK   ⓘ
The **Kew Greenhouse**, which was once the village bakery, has a quaint, refined atmosphere and serves steak pie, flans, quiches, Scotch beef and vegetarian dishes to a background of classical music. If it's a fine day, there are plenty of riverside pubs such as the **Town Wharf** and the **London Apprentice**, to choose from halfway through the walk.

# Deer Old Richmond Park

*A walking safari through Europe's largest city park, Richmond Park.*

| | |
|---|---|
| •DISTANCE• | 6¾ miles (10.9km) |
| •MINIMUM TIME• | 2hrs 30min |
| •ASCENT / GRADIENT• | 164ft (50m) |
| •LEVEL OF DIFFICULTY• | |
| •PATHS• | Mainly tarmac paths |
| •LANDSCAPE• | Parkland and deer |
| •SUGGESTED MAP• | aqua3 OS Explorer 161 London South |
| •START / FINISH• | Grid reference: TQ189728; Richmond Station (tube and rail) 1½ miles (2.4km) |
| •DOG FRIENDLINESS• | Will love it but keep on lead near deer |
| •PARKING• | Car park at Pembroke Lodge in Richmond Park |
| •PUBLIC TOILETS• | Pembroke Lodge |

## BACKGROUND TO THE WALK

Richmond Park was once a royal hunting ground and, even today, it retains this upper crust image. Covering 2,500 acres (1,013 ha), it is a wonderful mix of panoramic views, wildlife havens and landscaped plantations, which are worth seeing in all seasons. For the most part, the walk follows the Tamsin Trail, a 7½ mile (12.1km) leisure path that runs around the perimeter of the park and that is for the sole use of walkers and cyclists.

The 750 or so deer are free to wander in the parkland, much of which has remained unchanged for centuries. Cars are allowed in certain areas of the park – it's not unusual for drivers to have to wait for a few minutes while a herd of deer crosses the road in front of them – but the best way to observe these beautiful creatures is on foot. There are two types of deer in the park – red and fallow deer. The males and females of red deer are stags and hinds, and of fallow deer are bucks and does. Red deer are indigenous to Britain, but fallow deer were introduced about 1,000 years ago. Norman hunters preferred the fallow for its grace and beauty.

Although there are enough plants to provide a nutritional diet for deer, acorns, horse chestnuts and sweet chestnuts also help to build up fat reserves during the winter months. During the rut (from September to November) the stags can often be seen fighting and herding the hinds into small breeding groups. Give them a wide berth if you pass them during the walk and keep your dog on a lead, to avoid alarming them. Culls, although the least favourite part of a gamekeeper's job, are necessary not only to prevent overgrazing but also to help maintain the park's reputation for having some of the best herds in the world.

If you see a bird that would look more at home in the sub-tropics than London, it's probably a ring-necked parakeet. These colourful birds, which have very long, pointed wings, were brought into Britain from Africa and India in the 1960s and sold as pets. Those that managed to escape began to breed successfully in the wild, and, despite the colder climate of Britain, their numbers are increasing. Noise from groups can sometimes be heard from the treetops in Richmond Park. They love to eat crab apples in summer and sycamore seeds during the rest of the year. Although they do not represent a problem to other birds, fruit growers may not be so fond of them.

GOLF COURSE

④ ROBIN HOOD GATE

Kingston Vale

A 3

A 308

⑤ ROEHAMPTON GATE

ADAM'S POND

▲ 38 White Lodge

▲ 44 RICHMOND PARK

-N-

DEER PARK

P

½ Mile

½ Mile

③

ISABELLA PLANTATION

HAMCROSS PLANTATION

② HAM GATE

Sidmouth Wood

TAMSIN TRAIL

B 353

① ▲ 56

⑥ RICHMOND GATE

THE WICK

Ⓐ KING HENRY VIII MOUND

P WC PEMBROKE LODGE

B 327 STAR AND GARTER HOME

PETERSHAM HOTEL

Petersham

A 307

CANYON RESTAURANT

Ⓑ RIVER THAMES

Richmond

PETERSHAM LODGE WOODS

Ⓓ

MELANCHOLY WALK

LOCK RD

Marble Hill Park

HAM HOUSE

Ham

A 3004

A 316

HAMMERTON'S FERRY

A 305

St Margaret's

EEL PIE ISLAND

HAM LANDS

Ⓒ TEDDINGTON LOCK

A 310

Walk 38

## Walk 38 **Directions**

① From the car park at **Pembroke Lodge** turn right to follow the **Tamsin Trail** in the general direction of **Ham Gate**. The path veers to the right and later runs close to the road.

② At a crossroads leading to Ham Gate, turn left past the **Hamcross Plantation**. At the next crossroads turn right to visit the **Isabella Plantation**, otherwise continue and turn left at the next main junction, before another plantation, and circle the wood clockwise along a wide track. Turn right at the next junction and follow the path to the end of the pond.

### WHILE YOU'RE THERE

The **Isabella Plantation** was originally planted with oaks in 1831, but it now has three large ponds, a stream, a collection of rare trees and some magnificent azaleas. You'll be surprised how many people don't know that this is here – and you can't blame the ones that do for not sharing their secret, as this is a very special place, especially in the early morning.

③ Turn right along a path between the two ponds and continue ahead, ignoring paths branching off that would lead you to a car park. After this, turn right and follow the road that swings to the left towards **Robin Hood Gate**. Deer are often spotted here but their coats give them good camouflage, especially against a background of bracken.

### WHAT TO LOOK FOR

In the formal garden of Pembroke Lodge is the highest point in the park, **Henry VIII Mound**. This prehistoric burial ground is not easy to find (take the higher path past the cottage) but well worth the effort, for here is a view of the dome of St Paul's Cathedral through a keyhole of holly. The cathedral may be 10 miles (16.1km) away from the avenue of sweet chestnuts in the park but this is better than any optical illusion, and the view is also conserved. The King was said to have stood on this mound while his second wife, Anne Boleyn, was being beheaded at the Tower of London.

④ Turn left at Robin Hood Gate. Follow the gravel path of the **Tamsin Trail** past the **Richmond Park Golf Course** and on to **Roehampton Gate**.

⑤ Continue over a footbridge and, after a further 500yds (457m), the path winds to the right of **Adam's Pond**, which is one of the watering holes used by the deer. Follow the path across the upper end of the park, past **Sheen Gate**, to **Richmond Gate**.

⑥ Turn left at **Richmond Gate** and continue along the path to reach **Pembroke Lodge** and the start of the walk.

### WHERE TO EAT AND DRINK

**Pembroke Lodge**, designed by Sir John Soane, was the childhood home of Bertrand Russell. Its views over west London towards Windsor are vast (although Windsor Castle is hard to spot). The tea room offers hot dishes and snacks and has seating outside on the terrace in fine weather. If you are on Walk 39, turn right at Point ⑧ for 650yds (594m). Just before Richmond Bridge is **Canyon**, where south west London meets Arizona. There is seating outside near a funky cactus terrace, complete with giant maple tree; entry is through two of the largest wooden doors this side of Phoenix. The menu includes chargrilled tuna, lamb cutlets and various salads. Sunday brunch is very popular.

# Onwards to Ham House

*Take this considerable extension for views of Ham House, a fine example of Stuart architecture.*

**See map and information panel for Walk 38**

| | |
|---|---|
| •DISTANCE• | 11 miles (17.7km) |
| •MINIMUM TIME• | 4hrs 30min |
| •ASCENT / GRADIENT• | 164ft (50m) ▲▲ ▲ |
| •LEVEL OF DIFFICULTY• | 🚶🚶 🚶🚶 🚶🚶 |

## Walk 39 Directions (Walk 38 option)

Leave the main route at Point ⑥. Leave the park at **Richmond Gate** and then cross **Star and Garter Hill**. Walk down past the Royal Star and Garter Home for ex-servicemen, then turn left when you get to **The Wick**, a large white house, into **Nightingale Lane**, Point Ⓐ.

Follow this lane as it swings to the right at the Petersham Hotel. When it meets **Petersham Road** cross to the other side and take the path on the left, beside a brick wall. This tarmac path runs alongside **Petersham Meadows** to the **River Thames**, Point Ⓑ.

Turn left and follow the path as it passes an island and, later, the nature reserve of **Petersham Lodge Woods**. At a signpost to Ham House is the site of the Hammerton's Ferry, a one-person show that operates all year (although only at weekends in winter). Continue past **Eel Pie Island** and on to **Ham Lands**, a wooded local nature reserve. Turn left just before the blue bridge at **Teddington Lock**, Point Ⓒ.

Cross over two roads and pass through a set of metal gates to go along a fenced footpath. Turn right then take the first left into **Lock Road**. Continue ahead over a junction along **The Common** (here a road), past a pond. Just before the road bends to the right, and after the last cottage on the left, is a white fence, Point Ⓓ.

Beside this fence is **Melancholy Walk**, a long, gravel path leading to Ham House, seen through a tunnel of trees. Now cared for by the National Trust, Ham House is a unique example of 17th-century fashion and power. It has hardly changed since the Duke and Duchess of Lauderdale decorated it during this period. The gardens have been restored to their former glory and remain one of the few formal gardens that escaped the landscape trend of the 18th century. The interior is lavish with a fine collection of period furniture, textiles and paintings, including some by van Dyke.

Continue along **The Common**, crossing at the pedestrian lights on to **Ham Gate Avenue**. Follow this all the way back to **Richmond Park**, to rejoin the **Tamsin Trail** and Walk 38 at Point ②.

# Scratchwood's Surprising Open Space

*An ideal point to stop and stretch the legs if you are driving along the A1 or about to join the M1.*

| | |
|---|---|
| •DISTANCE• | 2 miles (3.2km) |
| •MINIMUM TIME• | 1hr |
| •ASCENT / GRADIENT• | 98ft (30m) ▲ ▲ ▲ |
| •LEVEL OF DIFFICULTY• | 🚶 🚶 🚶 |
| •PATHS• | Gravel paths and forest tracks |
| •LANDSCAPE• | Woodland |
| •SUGGESTED MAP• | aqua3 OS Explorer 173 London North |
| •START / FINISH• | Grid reference: TQ 207949 |
| •DOG FRIENDLINESS• | No problems |
| •PARKING• | Car park off northbound carriageway of A1, 1 mile (1.6km) north of Apex Corner |
| •PUBLIC TOILETS• | At car park |

## Walk 40 Directions

As you'll see from the information board, there are three marked trails here: red, blue and yellow. You can choose your own route or follow this one, which is a combination of the red and blue trails.

Head for the track at the far, right-hand corner of the car park, near the kiosk, and follow this path, part of the **London Loop**, through a metal gate. Take the right-hand fork, cross a footbridge over a ditch and follow the path uphill along the central path ahead.

The ancient woodland of Scratchwood can be traced back to the last Ice Age, when it was part of the Middlesex Forest. Although it first appeared on maps from the 16th century, other documents name it at least 300 years before that. Many landowners built large

houses in the area. In 1866 the Cox family bought a 1,000 acre (405ha) estate, which included Scratchwood. The area was used for game-rearing and field sports. Later the woodland management focused on producing oak timber. The relatively small woodland area of Scratchwood that you see today is mostly a result of the incursion of the A1 Barnet bypass, which, in 1927, sliced through the site separating it from Moat Mount, on the opposite side of the dual carriageway.

A few paces further on, the path swings to the right and then descends, crossing another path and a footbridge before dipping and ascending once more. Follow the path to the right as it crosses another footbridge. About 50yds (46m) further, at a wooden post marked red, turn left along a path that later narrows and descends gradually. Here you will see large clumps of rhododendron. These were introduced, but, given half a chance, grow at a tremendous speed and have a tendency to eliminate all other ground vegetation. Careful woodland management, undertaken by Barnet borough council, has been necessary to enable other species to survive. Elsewhere the ancient ground cover – such as bracken, bramble and ivy – can be seen. Most of the large trees in these woods are oaks, but you will also see other typical English woodland trees including hornbeam, hazel, birch, holly and wild cherry.

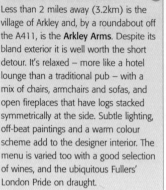

> **WHERE TO EAT AND DRINK** ⓘ
> Less than 2 miles away (3.2km) is the village of Arkley and, by a roundabout off the A411, is the **Arkley Arms**. Despite its bland exterior it is well worth the short detour. It's relaxed – more like a hotel lounge than a traditional pub – with a mix of chairs, armchairs and sofas, and open fireplaces that have logs stacked symmetrically at the side. Subtle lighting, off-beat paintings and a warm colour scheme add to the designer interior. The menu is varied too with a good selection of wines, and the ubiquitous Fullers' London Pride on draught.

> **WHILE YOU'RE THERE** ⓘ
> If you are a **model plane** enthusiast, take yours with you for the route takes you past a field where model aircraft are sometimes flown. The grass is kept short, by a combination of rabbits and mowing.

At a clearing leading down to an embankment, turn left. A little further on you'll pass more wooden posts, marked blue. As the path rises again bear sharp left at another post and turn right down steps and over a brook. Continue ahead as the path rises to another post and some more steps leading to a footbridge.

If you are walking here in the summer, you may hear the call of a jay. You may also catch the sound of a woodpecker – three different types have been spotted in Scratchwood. There have also been regular sightings of nuthatches and treecreepers on the tree trunks. The rough, bushy areas attract warblers and, in winter, redwings feed on berries. Insects too are attracted by the wide variety of habitats in Scratchwood, where on bright, sunny days you will see large numbers of butterflies and dragonflies. Be careful not to tread on any of the giant stag beetles you may see scuttling across the path; they are now a protected species.

The path passes three more posts and after the last, it rejoins the **London Loop**. The field to the south of the entrance was once a hay meadow, used for feeding some of London's large number of horses. At the footbridge, turn right along the limestone scalpings track back to the car park.

> **WHAT TO LOOK FOR** ⓘ
> Spare a thought for London's **woodlands** while walking through Scratchwood. For 5,000 years tree numbers fell consistently, making way for farms and land to grow crops. But, due to increased industrialisation and a shift towards city living, England now has as many trees as it did in the time of Robin Hood. That's roughly 25 trees for every man, woman and child in the country. The devastation seen after the 1987 storms made many people realise how much they took the landscape for granted. In fact, earlier in the 1980s the Forestry Commission was spending just £800,000 per year on planting new trees, but by 2000 this had risen to £9.7m. Robin Hood's merry men wouldn't find it difficult to hide in this area of woodland.

# Up and Over the Hill at Horsenden

*Some of London's best grassland and its wildlife are to be found on this walk with an extensive view.*

| | |
|---|---|
| •DISTANCE• | 2¾ miles (4.4km) |
| •MINIMUM TIME• | 1hr 30min |
| •ASCENT / GRADIENT• | 180ft (55m) ▲▲▲ |
| •LEVEL OF DIFFICULTY• | 🚶🚶 🚶🚶 🚶🚶 |
| •PATHS• | Mainly woodland tracks |
| •LANDSCAPE• | Woods, meadows, tow path and extensive views |
| •SUGGESTED MAP• | aqua3 OS Explorer 173 London North |
| •START / FINISH• | Grid reference: TQ 162845; add 650yds (594m) if joining the walk from Perivale tube at Point ⑤ |
| •DOG FRIENDLINESS• | No particular problems |
| •PARKING• | Car park at Horsenden Hill |
| •PUBLIC TOILETS• | None on route |

## BACKGROUND TO THE WALK

The summit of Horsenden Hill sits 276 feet (84m) above suburban west London, making it one of the highest points in the capital. It is also the largest open space in the Borough of Ealing. At one time this area was dense woodland where wild boar, bears and wolves roamed, but now the wildlife is much less aggressive. If you like a hill to be a hill and want a steeper uphill walk for a better workout, do this route in reverse. (Reversing the directions will tax your brain a little more too!)

### Heading for Colour

The best time to see the diversity of wild flowers and invertebrates, such as butterflies, is from June to August, when Horsenden Hill is transformed into a landscape of colour. Small copper and common blue butterflies are often seen in the area by the series of steep steps leading down to the solitary oak tree, because their caterpillars like to feed on plants from the dock and pea family, which grow here in abundance. Dyer's greenweed also thrives here, although the plant is quite scarce in London. Its yellow extract was once used to dye cloth and was mixed with a blue extract from the woad plant to make a green dye.

Unlike most agricultural grasslands that have been fertilised and sprayed with herbicides, the grasslands here have simply been left to develop naturally, first by grazing and then by hay cutting. In this way, wild flowers have prospered.

### Conservation in the Woodland

The traditional methods of cultivating the land also extend to the woodland. A good example of this is the ancient Perivale Wood, which becomes a sea of bluebells in spring. As you walk along the canal beside the wood you may notice that some of the willows have been cut to a height of about 7ft (2m), or 'pollarded'. This management technique ensured that when new shoots grew they were out of reach of cattle. Now it provides a habitat for beetles and other insects. It makes a good nesting area and food supply for birds, too. Lichen is growing on some of the tree trunks, which is an indication of good air quality because the organism, a mix of algae and a fungus, can only grow successfully in clean air. Although rangers are sometimes accused of felling trees unnecessarily, it is an important part of woodland management since it means that trees do not have to fight for light. There remain many 'standards' in the woodland – oak trees that have been left to grow for more than 100 years. Another conservation technique carried out is the old craft of hedge laying. The slim trunks of the hedging trees are partly cut (but not severed), then bent over to allow new growth to appear from the stump. The extra sunlight allows flowers such as cow parsley and red campion to grow at ground level.

**Walk 41**

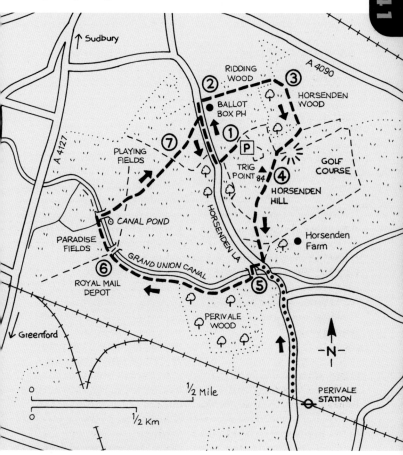

## Walk 41 **Directions**

① From the car park walk back towards the road. At the metal barrier turn right down some steps and continue along a tarmac path that runs parallel to Horsenden

Lane. Continue in front of the **Ballot Box** pub to reach a tarmac path just past it.

② Turn right along this tree-lined path and keep ahead as it passes **Ridding Wood** on the left. After ¼ mile (400m) turn right, just

Walk 41

before a metal gate and a row of houses, to enter **Horsenden Wood**.

③ Within a few paces take the left-hand path at a fork and keep ahead as it climbs steadily uphill then crosses a tarmac path. Bear right at the row of trees ahead of you that marks the boundary of the **golf course**. When the ground levels towards the top of the hill, go to the **viewpoint** ahead on the left.

**WHERE TO EAT AND DRINK**

The **Ballot Box** pub takes its name from a hotel that once stood 300yds (274m) south of the present building. This was where boatmen in the 19th century voted after walking from the nearest canal, about 600yds (549m) away. Lunch is served all day and the pub has a family dining section and an indoor play area for children.

④ Head for the triangulation pillar behind the viewpoint in the middle of the grassy plateau. Take the footpath on the far right that leads to a flight of steep, wooden steps going into a thickly wooded area. Continue down the steps. At a crossing of paths keep ahead, passing to the left of a solitary oak tree, to reach the road.

⑤ Turn left to cross a footbridge over the **Grand Union Canal** (Paddington Branch). Just after this turn left again, down some steps, to the tow path. Continue under the bridge along this peaceful stretch of

**WHILE YOU'RE THERE**

Take a look at **Paradise Fields**, a newly developed area of agricultural land to the rear of the wooden bridge crossed after Point ⑥. There's a lake that attracts lapwings and swans. Other wildlife includes, snipe, linnet and goldfinches, and foxes. On the opposite side of the bridge, Canal Pond provides a wetland habitat for dragonflys. Common terns are often seen fishing near here and herons are regular visitors in winter.

the canal, which later widens and passes **Perivale Wood** (and the neighbouring Royal Mail postal services depot).

⑥ Keep walking straight ahead for another ¼ mile (400m). Turn left after a wooden footbridge to go through a kissing gate. Carry on over the bridge (Horsenden Hill is now visible again in front of you) and follow the winding footpath to go through another kissing gate. Turn left along a footpath to the right of some playing fields and continue ahead.

⑦ At the end of the fields bear right to go through a gap in the trees, then turn left over a footbridge and keep to the right edge of the next meadow. Keep going towards another meadow and head for the building beyond its left diagonal corner, the **Ballot Box** pub. Cross the road and turn right to retrace your steps along the tarmac path to return to the start.

**WHAT TO LOOK FOR**

If the weather is hot then you'll notice that the ground has wide shrinkage cracks, whereas after rain it becomes waterlogged and muddy. Blame this on the geology of Horsenden Hill and the thickness of **London Clay** here. The difficulty of working this soil was the main reason for the change in agricultural practices in the 19th century when wheat growing (to make flour) was largely replaced by hay production (to feed animals). Walk in this clinging mud on a rainy London day and you may feel some sympathy for the ploughman of old.

# Admiring the Marvel of Osterley

*A look at the outstanding achievements of Isambard Kingdom Brunel, whose work led to improved transport.*

| | |
|---|---|
| •DISTANCE• | 5 miles (8km) |
| •MINIMUM TIME• | 2hrs 30min |
| •ASCENT / GRADIENT• | 66ft (20m) |
| •LEVEL OF DIFFICULTY• | |
| •PATHS• | Mixture of tow paths, tarmac paths and rough tracks |
| •LANDSCAPE• | Farmland, canal boats, locks and a landscaped park |
| •SUGGESTED MAP• | aqua3 OS Explorer 161 London South |
| •START / FINISH• | Grid reference: TQ 148779; Osterley tube ¾mile (1.2km) |
| •DOG FRIENDLINESS• | On lead except in designated 'off-lead' areas |
| •PARKING• | Car park in Osterley Park (free to National Trust members) |
| •PUBLIC TOILETS• | Osterley Park |

## BACKGROUND TO THE WALK

The Industrial Revolution was a period of remarkable growth. It took off in the mid-1700s, when the domestic cottage industries were gradually replaced by large factories that provided work for hundreds of people. By 1850 Britain had become the first country in the world with a predominantly industrial, urban work force. It was a time of vast development, during which Isambard Kingdom Brunel played a major role.

### The Age of Travel
Brunel was born in Portsmouth in 1806, at the height of the Industrial Revolution. Although he was a small man – he wore top hats to appear taller – the sky was the limit as far as his work as an engineer was concerned. At that time canals were the motorways of the country. Although snail-like by today's standards, one of their great innovations had been the horse-drawn barge, because it could carry a 50 ton load compared to the 300lb (136kg) capability of a horse and cart. The first section of the Grand Union Canal was opened in 1794. This walk passes two points of particular interest along it. The Hanwell Flight of six locks is an impressive 'staircase' that raises the canal 53ft (16m) in just over 600yds (549m). Three Bridges, although belonging to the railway age, also involves the canal. Here Brunel contrived a unique construction where rail, road and canal all cross each other.

### Dreams Do Come True
Until the arrival of the railway, passenger travel was uncomfortable and very slow because the roads used by horse-drawn carriages were often uneven and muddy. But Brunel pioneered an alternative when, together with Robert Stephenson and Joseph Locke, he helped design the world's first railway network. Brunel's contribution was the Great Western Railway between London and Bristol, a broad gauge line which was noted for its elegant bridges, stations and viaducts. Although financed by the movement of freight, it also put long-distance passenger travel within the reach of ordinary people.

During this inspirational phase of British history Brunel also found time to design steamships, one of which became a prototype for all future ocean liners. The first, the largest ship ever built at the time, was intended to revolutionise trans-Atlantic travel in the same way that railways had transformed inland communication. His third, the *Great Eastern*, aimed at making a round-trip to Australia via the Cape of Good Hope without having to refuel with coal. The ship was so large that it took months to move it from its base and, unfortunately, because Australian trade slumped around this time, the project was deemed a financial flop. Despite this, the *Great Eastern* is remembered as the ship that laid the first successful sub-Atlantic telegraph cable, thereby hugely improving links with North America. It wasn't the first of Brunel's extravagant projects to fail, but he was a determined man with a huge dream and his legacy as an engineering genius remains unparalleled.

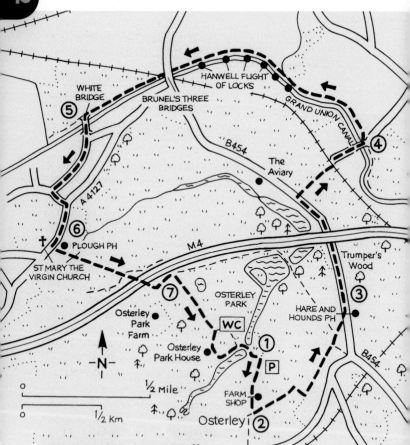

# Walk 42 **Directions**

① From the car park in Osterley Park, walk back along the track heading towards the entrance gates, passing a **farm shop**.

② Just past the shop, and opposite a bungalow, turn left through a gate and later another, to follow a track between fields. When the path ends bear left towards a brick wall, cross a track and continue to the pub, the **Hare and Hounds**.

In the next mile (1.6km) you will pass the **Hanwell Flight** of six locks and then Brunel's remarkable **Three Bridges** construction.

⑤ Cross the white bridge ahead of you and continue walking along **Melbury Avenue**. When you reach the T-junction turn left and then right at the mini-roundabout.

③ Turn left along the road to pass under the **M4**. After a further 440yds (402m), just past a building on your left, turn right to go through a kissing gate and follow an enclosed path alongside a playing field. At the end of the path go through a metal gate to your right, then cross the railway line and follow the road ahead.

④ Past the bridge, go down the steps on the right to the **Grand Union Canal**, then turn right under the bridge, along the tow path.

⑥ Turn left along an enclosed public footpath, signposted to **St Mary's Avenue**, beside the **Plough** pub. Cross the road and continue along the footpath opposite, which crosses a field. At the far side of the field climb the steps and follow the road over the **M4** motorway.

⑦ Ignoring the first metal gate along this road, turn right through the second one to re-enter **Osterley Park**. Keep going along this straight track, through farmland and an avenue of small-leaved lime trees, to reach a metal gate. Go past some stable buildings and the main house, then take the path around the pond to reach the car park where the walk began.

# Anyone for Real Tennis at Hampton Court?

*Discover more about the game of kings on a walk through the regal landscape of Hampton Court Park.*

| | |
|---|---|
| •DISTANCE• | 4¾ miles (7.7km) |
| •MINIMUM TIME• | 1hr 45min |
| •ASCENT / GRADIENT• | Negligible |
| •LEVEL OF DIFFICULTY• | |
| •PATHS• | Gravel, tarmac and riverside tracks |
| •LANDSCAPE• | Landscaped grounds of historic palace |
| •SUGGESTED MAP• | aqua3 OS Explorer 161 London South |
| •START / FINISH• | Grid reference: TQ 174697; Hampton Court rail |
| •DOG FRIENDLINESS• | Keep dogs under control near deer |
| •PARKING• | Car park in Hampton Court Road |
| •PUBLIC TOILETS• | Hampton Court Park |

## BACKGROUND TO THE WALK

The majority of visitors to Hampton Court come to see the state apartments of William III and Henry VIII, the Tudor kitchens and perhaps the maze and the 60 acres (24ha) of riverside gardens. Most miss the subtle doorway in the wall that looks like the opening to a secret garden. In fact it is the entrance to one of the more unusual parts of the palace, and the most historic court in the world – the real tennis court.

### Courting a Historic Ball Game

The Royal Tennis Court at Hampton Court has serious royal connections. Henry VIII played real tennis here as did Charles I. Today Prince Edward and his wife, Sophie, are two of the club's 700 members. Cardinal Wolsey built the original real tennis court in the 1520s on the site of the present Stuart court, but it remained roofless until 1636. During the Second World War it was once again roofless, when a bomb hit the adjacent apartments and completely shattered the court's windows.

Apart from 'real tennis', any of the terms 'royal tennis', 'court tennis' and 'close tennis' may be used to distinguish this ancient game from the more familiar 'lawn tennis' (although that is rarely played on a lawn nowadays). The game, from which many other ball games – such as table tennis and squash – are derived, was probably being played as early as the 6th century BC. The word 'tennis' stems from the French 'tenez' or the Anglo-French 'tenetz' which translates as 'take it', referring to what the server might call to their opponent. Although the game was originally played outside, it may have moved to an enclosed court for reasons of privacy and, pragmatically, to avoid the filthy streets in the Middle Ages. The game was very popular in France with the aristocracy but suffered considerably for this association during the revolution. After the First World War it declined in popularity in England, but it has seen a revival lately. At least one notable health club now has a real tennis court and Middlesex University has recently spent £1.5 million building a state-of-the-art court at its Hendon campus.

**Walk 43**

### The Unconventional Chase

If you're a real tennis novice then the court will probably look like a cross between a badminton court and a medieval street roof. Yet it's a quirky game to watch, for the serve can be over or underarm as long as the ball bounces at least once on the roof (known as a penthouse) and then on the floor within the service court. The rackets are shaped more like a buckled bicycle tyre than a conventional tennis racket but the game is fast, energetic and skilful. Although there are some similarities to lawn tennis, the main difference lies in the 'chase'. Initially, this seems like a complicated manoeuvre and it is best understood by watching players in action but it comes into play when the ball bounces twice in certain areas of the court. The world champion, Rob Fahey, admits to having been initially attracted more by the glitzy parties than the game itself, but the sport has grown in stature over the past few years and seems now to have the ball firmly back in its own court.

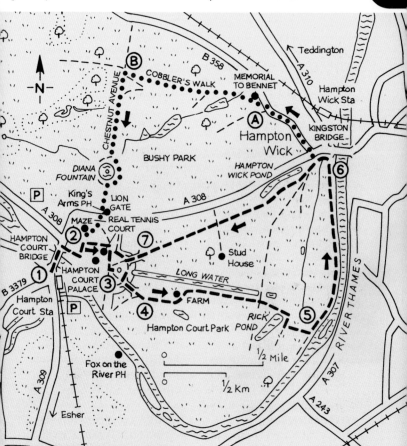

## Walk 43 Directions

① Cross **Hampton Court Bridge**, turn right through the main gates to **Hampton Court Palace** and walk along a wide drive. Just before the palace turn left through the gatehouse and then under an arch.

② Turn right just before the tea room, through a gateway along a

**Walk 43**

path through gardens. At the end, on the right, is the real tennis court building. Pass through another gateway and turn sharp right to walk alongside the real tennis court and past the entrance to it.

③ Take the central gravel path in front of the palace, past the fountain to the ornate railings overlooking the **Long Water**, an artificial lake nearly ¾ mile (1.2km) in length. Head towards the footbridge on the right and go through the wrought-iron gates.

④ After 220yds (201m) the footpath bears left and joins a tarmac track. Follow this, turning left by some farm buildings, after which the path runs parallel to the **Long Water**. Where the lake ends continue ahead at a crossing of tracks and bear right to skirt the left side of **Rick Pond**. Turn left

through a metal gate, along an enclosed footpath and through a gate to reach the **River Thames**.

⑤ Turn left along this riverside path and follow it for ¾ mile (1.2km) to **Kingston Bridge**. Here, join the road leading to the roundabout.

⑥ At the end of the row of houses turn left through a gateway. Immediately after the cattle grid bear right along a grassy path running along the left side of the boomerang-shaped **Hampton Wick Pond**. Follow the straight path for about ¾ mile (1.2km) back to **Hampton Court Palace**.

⑦ Bear right to cross a footbridge and follow the footpath back to the real tennis court, from where you can retrace your steps to the start of the walk over **Hampton Court Bridge** and back into **Hampton Court Road**.

# Where a Bushy Park Cobbler Won a Right of Way

*A longer circuit through Bushy Park, following the footsteps of a local cobbler.*
**See map and information panel for Walk 43**

| | |
|---|---|
| •**DISTANCE**• | 6¾ miles (10.9km) |
| •**MINIMUM TIME**• | 2hrs 45min |
| •**ASCENT / GRADIENT**• | Negligible |
| •**LEVEL OF DIFFICULTY**• | 𝕩𝕩 𝕩𝕩 𝕩𝕩 |

## Walk 44 **Directions** (Walk 43 option)

Leave Walk 43 at Point ⑥ and cross the road at the traffic lights into **Grove Road**, as the road curves to the left it becomes **Park Road**. Continue, then, just before the road swings to the right, enter Bushy Park through the metal gates, Point Ⓐ. At the gate you'll see the memorial to Timothy Bennet.

Timothy Bennet had a shoemaker's shop in Hampton Wick in the 18th century. Market days usually kept Bennet on his toes but he gradually noticed that, instead of passing his shop on the way to Kingston market, people were going the long way round by the road. When he discovered that the park ranger, the Earl of Halifax, had closed the footpath going through Bushy Park, he was determined to do something about it, not least because he was losing business. He committed the enormous sum of £700 to pay his legal costs and served notice on the peer that he intended to establish a public right of way. At first Halifax was dismissive of the claim, but public

and political opinion was as fickle then as it is now. He decided there would be more public relations mileage in relenting than in being seen to be taken on by, and possibly losing in court to, a mere cobbler. Timothy Bennet died two years after his success, aged 77, in 1754 and the path through Bushy Park was later named Cobbler's Walk in his honour.

Take the path on the right and continue along **Cobbler's Walk**, ignoring the path that joins it a few paces further. Cross a brook. When you reach the buildings on the left take the grassy path skirting the fence to the house. Ignoring the first tarmac path, take the second path on the right, which heads towards the road and away from the house. At the road turn left along **Chestnut Avenue**, Point Ⓑ.

At the **Diana Fountain** follow the path round to the left and through the park gates. Cross **Hampton Court Road** and go through **Lion Gate** opposite, to re-enter Hampton Court Park. At a meeting of paths bear right, to pass to the left of the maze. Turn left at a T-junction turn and, where a set of paths cross, rejoin the Walk 43 at Point ②.

# Brent River Park

*A walk along the meandering River Brent with its adjacent meadows and colonies of bats.*

Walk 45

| | |
|---|---|
| •DISTANCE• | 3½ miles (5.7km) |
| •MINIMUM TIME• | 2hrs 45min |
| •ASCENT / GRADIENT• | Negligible |
| •LEVEL OF DIFFICULTY• | |
| •PATHS• | Mainly grassy riverside tracks that can get muddy |
| •LANDSCAPE• | Riverside meadows and wildlife |
| •SUGGESTED MAP• | aqua3 OS Explorer 173 London North |
| •START | Grid reference: TQ 153805; Hanwell rail |
| FINISH• | Grid reference: TQ 163832; Perivale tube |
| •DOG FRIENDLINESS• | Not allowed in churchyard |
| •PARKING• | Plenty in streets adjacent to Hanwell rail |
| •PUBLIC TOILETS• | Brent Lodge Park |
| •NOTE• | To return to start, take 95 bus from Western Avenue to Greenford Red Lion, then E3 to Hanwell station |

## Walk 45 Directions

From **Hanwell railway station** follow the road in front as it bends to the left. At the end turn left and head towards the viaduct. Just before it, cross the road and join a tarmac path to the left of a small, enclosed recreation ground. A few paces further on take the paved path on the left and continue as it becomes a track running beside the

> **WHILE YOU'RE THERE** ⓘ
> Take a look at the **Millennium Maze** in Brent Lodge Park – follow the path to the right of the steps. It was created using 2,000 young yews on the site of an old bowling green and emphasises just how slowly these trees grow. Yews are ideal for borders and mazes as they are easy to prune. Today, they have a role in cancer treatment – an extract derived from their crushed leaves is used to produce drugs which inhibit cells from dividing and spreading the disease.

**Wharncliffe Viaduct**. Isambard Kingdom Brunel designed the viaduct in 1837 and it was used by the Great Western Railway to carry trains from London to Bristol.

Enter the gates to **Brent Lodge Park** and go up the steps to your left, past the fingerpost signed 'Brent River Park'. At the end of the meadows follow the path through the trees as it runs alongside the river. Continue across the grass, past **St Mary's Church** on your right, and go down a set of steps then through a wooden gate. The area ahead is where the colonies of bats often feed.

Many of these warm-blooded mammals hang from the nooks and crannies of Wharncliffe Viaduct, coming out at dusk to feed on insects along the river. You won't see them in winter though, as this is when they hibernate, due to lack of food supplies.

Walk 45

Cross the iron bridge to take the right-hand path. Just a few paces further take a right-hand fork to join the riverside track. When this meets another, turn right and head towards the footbridge. Cross it and turn left across a footbridge over a ditch – carry on, with the river on your left. Keep ahead at the next bridge to join a prominent path. At the next fork turn left. Now carry on past a wooden bridge and then go to the right of an extended area of reed beds.

> **WHERE TO EAT AND DRINK** ℹ
> The view of the viaduct from Hanwell Bridge on the Uxbridge Road is spectacular and it just so happens that the Fuller's **Viaduct** pub is strategically placed near the bridge. Otherwise, for something completely different, turn left before the footbridge in Western Avenue to find **Starvin Marvin's Diner** for a big, American, all-day breakfast.

The reed beds here provide not only nesting sites for reed warblers but also feeding areas for migrating birds, especially in autumn. On the opposite bank you'll see willows that have been traditionally pollarded. They resemble enormous tufted bulbs sprouting from the top of the trunk.

Continue ahead past a weir. Behind the steep bank on your right is the **Bridge Avenue Extension**. If the riverside track is muddy then head for the grassy path at the top. Keep ahead to the left of a sports field. At the end cross **Ruislip Road** and join a path on the left, signposted 'Brent River Park Walk'.

After two more weirs, the second of which is enclosed by railings, you will see **Perivale Golf Course** on the left. Continue on this path as it

runs parallel to the road and merges with the pavement for 20yds (18m) before veering to the left under the railway bridge. After a metal footbridge go up some wooden steps. Pass to the left of **Gurnell Sports Centre** and bear left along a narrow, gently descending track, following the river along the edge of the sports field.

After the sports field turn left, towards **Argyle Road**. Turn right here until you reach the traffic lights. Cross the road and turn left along a tarmac path signposted to **Perivale Lane**. At a crossing of paths keep ahead along a fenced path that slices through **Ealing Golf Course**. At the end turn left to cross a wooden bridge. Ahead is the white-timbered steeple of the 12th-century **St Mary the Virgin Church** in Perivale, whose churchyard is a haven for wildlife and features the rare black poplar tree. The church is now an arts centre and holds plays and concerts during summer weekends.

At the lychgate turn left and then right into **Old Church Lane**. At the end cross the footbridge over the busy **Western Avenue** to reach **Perivale** tube.

> **WHAT TO LOOK FOR** ℹ
> If you're out walking in the afternoon you may see some of the colonies of **pipistrelle bats** that have set up home in the brickwork of Wharncliffe Viaduct. This species, London's commonest bat, is so small that it can fit into a matchbox. It flies up to treetop height, searching for tasty midges to eat. In the fading light they locate food by sending out high-pitched sounds that echo back, giving them information about the location of their prey. As walkers' heads are not on their menu, they will probably do everything they can to avoid you.

Walk 46

# The Literary Highs of Harrow on the Hill

*A circular walk around Harrow on the Hill where Lord Byron and Anthony Trollope went to school.*

| | |
|---|---|
| •DISTANCE• | 3½ miles (5.7km) |
| •MINIMUM TIME• | 2hrs |
| •ASCENT / GRADIENT• | 213ft (65m) ▲▲▲ |
| •LEVEL OF DIFFICULTY• | 🚶🚶 🚶 |
| •PATHS• | Footpath, fields and pavements |
| •LANDSCAPE• | Hilltop views and buildings of Harrow School |
| •SUGGESTED MAP• | aqua3 OS Explorer 173 London North |
| •START / FINISH• | Grid reference: TQ 153880; Harrow-on-the-Hill tube |
| •DOG FRIENDLINESS• | No problems |
| •PARKING• | Pay-and-display in nearby streets. |
| •PUBLIC TOILETS• | None on route |

## BACKGROUND TO THE WALK

From a humble start in 1572, when local farmer John Lyon obtained a royal charter, Harrow has become one of the country's best-known boys' schools. During the walk you will tread the same ground as Anthony Trollope and Lord Byron who, although both distinguished writers, had very different journeys through life.

### Poetic Licence

Lord Byron was only ten years old when he inherited his title in 1798, and he started school at Harrow in 1801. Although his classmates remembered him best for his satire and wit, he could be a sensitive and reflective child – he would sit in the churchyard for hours.

> '*Spot of my youth, whose hoary branches sigh,*
> *Swept by the breeze that fans thy cloudless sky*'

However, by the time he left for Cambridge University in 1805 he had grown into a handsome man and had no shortage of female admirers. These included Lady Caroline Lamb, with whom he had an affair. But Byron also concealed a grave secret – his father had a daughter, Augusta, from a previous marriage. Byron had met Augusta for the first time when he was only 14, but when they met again nine years later, they became constant and very close companions. In due course she became pregnant and gave birth to a daughter. The following year Byron married Annabella Milbanke, but she later left him and rumours of his possible incest with Augusta soon spread. His friends and public turned against him. A deeply embittered Byron left England for Europe, never to return. His mistress, Claire, gave birth to a daughter, Allegra, who is buried in the churchyard of St Mary's. Later, he became involved in the struggle for democracy in Italy and Greece. In 1821 he had his most productive year yet, completing *Don Juan* and *The Vision of Judgement,* but he was just 36 years old when he died from a fever in Greece.

**A Man of Letters**

School days were not the happiest times of Anthony Trollope's life because a decline in the family fortune prompted a move from a rather grand house in Harrow to a farmhouse in Harrow Weald. After leaving school he joined the General Post Office (GPO), but it wasn't until a transfer to Ireland seven years later that Trollope's career really took off. One of his achievements was to introduce the pillar box to Great Britain.

By the time he decided to leave the GPO to concentrate on writing, Trollope was already an accomplished novelist. He had disciplined himself to write from 5:30AM until breakfast, after which he left for work. Although his skills weren't recognised until his fourth novel, *The Warden* (1855), was published, he became a prolific author (47 novels), including the 'Barsetshire' series and *The Way We Live Now* (1875).

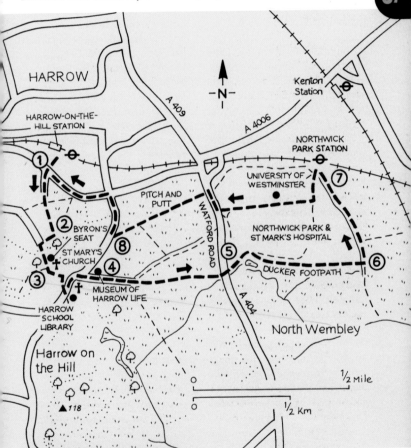

## Walk 46 Directions

① Follow the signs for the Lowlands Road exit of **Harrow-on-the-Hill Station** and cross the road at the pedestrian crossing. Turn left and then right, up **Lansdowne Road**. At the top of this follow the public footpath ahead, signposted 'The Hill'.

② Before the trees, turn right along an enclosed footpath. At a road turn

**Walk 46**

left, uphill again, along a tarmac path beside a churchyard. (Here, you can follow the crescent-shaped path to the right and climb the steep path at the end, or continue ahead to reach **St Mary's Church**.)

③ Leave by the lychgate and turn right, along **Church Hill**. At the bottom turn sharp left and cross the road towards the **school library** and church. Follow the road as it swings to the right after the church.

④ Turn right along **Football Lane** and pick up a footpath signposted to **Watford Road**. At the end of the school buildings keep ahead along a path leading downhill, to reach the playing fields. Take a look back here at Harrow School and the church spires. Follow the footpath sign pointing diagonally to the left across the field (not the one that follows the tarmac path to the left) to reach a stile leading to the busy **Watford Road**. Cross this with care.

⑤ Pick up **The Ducker Footpath** opposite and carry on ahead as it passes close to **Northwick Park Hospital**, before veering to the right, across the grass.

⑥ When you get to the end of the hospital buildings, turn left along a tarmac path beside a brook, with playing fields to your right. At the end of this long path is **Northwick Park tube**.

> **WHERE TO EAT AND DRINK** ⓘ
> Take a short detour along the High Street from the school library where you will find three eateries – the **French Bistro**, **Gaucho's Pizza and Pasta** and **Tea At Three**, a quaint teashop near to Harrow School's outfitters.

⑦ Turn left just before the tube station, along a footpath which passes two chimneys. Follow this as it veers to the right and passes between the buildings of Northwick Park Hospital and the University of Westminster campus. At the end of the footpath turn left. Cross the busy **A404** at the traffic lights. Turn right to follow the dual carriageway for 100yds (91m) and go through a gate along an enclosed footpath running by the side of a pitch-and-putt golf course.

> **WHILE YOU'RE THERE** ⓘ
> During term-time on Sundays the **Museum of Harrow Life** is open to the public. Although compact, it is packed with history about the school. It shows what a boy's room is like, explains about the boarding houses and their colours, famous Old Boys and the sports and activities that take place. There's also a small gift shop.

⑧ At the end of this straight, long footpath turn right along **Peterborough Road**, then left to reach **Lowlands Road**. Harrow-on-the-Hill Station is on your right.

> **WHAT TO LOOK FOR** ⓘ
> In the churchyard of **St Mary's Church** you'll notice a plaque pointing out the place where Byron loved to sit as a schoolboy. It was certainly a seat with a commanding view, looking towards Windsor. He would spend hours here, finding it the perfect place to reflect. You can see how London's suburbs have swallowed up vast areas of countryside to the north and west. In Byron's day this view would have been one of never-ending farmland and heath. Most of the sprawling development you see now dates from the earlier part of the 20th century. Byron's daughter, Allegra, who died at the age of five, is buried here in an unmarked grave.

# No Surrender in Wartime Harrow Weald

*Circling the boundaries of Bentley Priory, a key wartime defence installation and still an important military base.*

| | |
|---|---|
| •DISTANCE• | 4 miles (6.4km) |
| •MINIMUM TIME• | 2hrs |
| •ASCENT / GRADIENT• | 197ft (60m) ▲▲▲ |
| •LEVEL OF DIFFICULTY• | 🚶 🚶 🚶 |
| •PATHS• | Clearly marked footpaths |
| •LANDSCAPE• | Mixture of pretty woodland trails and open fields |
| •SUGGESTED MAP• | aqua3 OS Explorer 173 London North |
| •START / FINISH• | Grid reference: TQ 158936; Stanmore tube 1½ miles (2.4km) |
| •DOG FRIENDLINESS• | No problems |
| •PARKING• | Car park off Warren Lane |
| •PUBLIC TOILETS• | None on route |

## BACKGROUND TO THE WALK

By the spring of 1940, German forces had penetrated Western Europe so extensively that only Britain stood in the way of the Nazis taking complete control of the continent. It became clear, however, that Adolf Hitler was up against one of the best air forces in the world, and Bentley Priory played a strategic part in this battle of land – and wits.

### Behind the Scenes at the Priory

Unlike the Royal Air Force airfields that were home to British fighter planes during the war, the land surrounding Bentley Priory was without aircraft, yet it was one of a number of such places that were vital to the success of RAF operations.

The former country mansion was taken over by the RAF in 1926. It was enlarged considerably before it became the headquarters of Fighter Command, a group of high-ranking officers and other personnel on whose shoulders rested the ultimate responsibility for defending the country. This elite unit was formed in 1936 as part of the RAF's reorganisation and expansion in Britain. It was further divided into a number of groups, each of which took responsibility for a particular region. At the beginning of the Battle of Britain, for example, London and the South East was covered by 11 Group. These groups were also sub-divided into geographical areas for additional precision.

Bentley Priory was the centre of a highly sophisticated control network that relayed information on hostile aircraft movements via secure landlines from the radar stations to its 'filter room'. Once the plots of hostile aircraft had been established, the relevant group was alerted and the sector stations then activated the fighter squadrons.

### Bentley's Role in the Battle of Britain

When, in 1940, German forces occupied the whole of the northern European seaboard, Britain braced itself for attack. The Luftwaffe knew that, to gain air superiority over southern England, it first needed to destroy the RAF's fighter planes. It was necessary to win control of the skies just long enough for land and sea forces to come ashore. The Battle of Britain, as it became known, ran from July to October. Initially the Luftwaffe attacked targets in the south, including radar stations, until it reached the airfields near to London in 11 Group. Sir Winston Churchill, who had become Prime Minister in May of that year, told the House of Commons that the battle of France was over and that he expected the battle of Britain to begin soon – it began one month after his remarks. The Battle of Britain was a close shave, with some of the vital airfields around London being struck, but the enemy made a tactical mistake in choosing to concentrate on the capital. A week later, Fighter Command had recovered sufficiently to prove its superior strength. Today, in peacetime, Bentley Priory remains important, monitoring the security of British airspace.

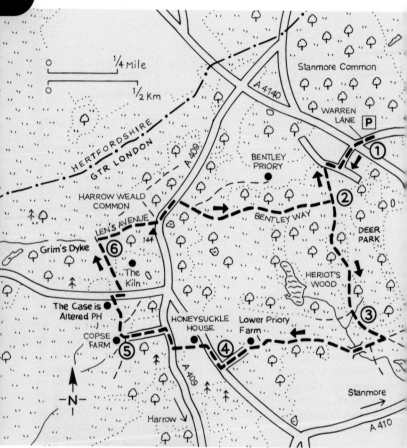

## Walk 47 Directions

① From the car park turn right, along **Warren Lane**. At the junction cross the road and continue ahead along **Priory Drive**. Follow the road

as it bends sharply to the right but, 50yds (43m) further on, go through a kissing gate on your left, signposted 'Bentley Way'. Continue along the track, with **Bentley Priory** to your right, and go through another kissing gate.

# Woods, Glorious Woods and a River

*Extend Walk 48 through more attractive woodland and follow the little River Pinn.*

**See map and information panel for Walk 48**

**Walk 49**

| | |
|---|---|
| •DISTANCE• | 5¾ miles (9.2km) |
| •MINIMUM TIME• | 3hrs |
| •ASCENT / GRADIENT• | 197ft (60m) ▲▲▲ |
| •LEVEL OF DIFFICULTY• | 🚶🚶🚶 |

## Walk 49 Directions (Walk 48 option)

Leave Walk 48 at Point ⑥ by turning left along a path, heading uphill. After it levels out, keep ahead at a crossing of paths to reach a more pronounced one ahead. Cross a brook and, after 100yds (91m), you'll notice a path to your right. Turn left here, Point Ⓐ.

Go on a few paces, to pick up the path ahead through the trees. Follow this until you reach a stile. Turn right across the grass to follow the wide, central path into the trees, where it then snakes before joining a road, Point Ⓑ. At a T-junction turn left into **Elmbridge Drive**. Just after the road bends to the right and before a bridge, turn right along a path heading towards a field. Follow this path across the meadow beside the little **River Pinn** and then a playing field, to leave via a metal gate on to a road, Point Ⓒ.

The name Ruislip is thought to have come from the words 'rush leap' indicating that at one time the River Pinn, which runs through the area, 'leapt' near rushes on the river bank. This part of the walk passes through suburban Ruislip. You'll follow the trail of the chuckling River Pinn as it runs alongside playing fields and houses.

Cross the road, then go through the metal gate opposite. Bear left and then right to join a footpath across the fields. After the footpath has run in a semi circle to the left, turn sharp right through a gap in the hedge to follow the **River Pinn** again. At the end of the meadow cross the road and follow the paved public footpath ahead until it reaches a road, Point Ⓓ.

Turn right along this road, **Sherwood Avenue**, then go over the crossroads. At a T-junction re-enter **Park Wood** via a metal gate. Keep ahead, then, at a fork, bear right. Now follow this path, ignoring any side paths. At a large crossing of paths keep ahead as your path bears slightly left to reach another, in front of the **Ruislip Lido**. Turn left here and then right, through gap in the fence, to reach Point ⑦ of Walk 48, from where you can return to the car park at **Young Wood** and the start of the walk.

Walk 50

# Harmondsworth Moor: Walkways Near Runways

*Relaxation for the whole family close to Heathrow Airport through an attractive area of regenerated land.*

| | |
|---|---|
| •DISTANCE• | 2¼ miles (3.6km) |
| •MINIMUM TIME• | 1hr 30min |
| •ASCENT / GRADIENT• | Negligible |
| •LEVEL OF DIFFICULTY• | |
| •PATHS• | Mainly gravel paths |
| •LANDSCAPE• | Green belt, rivers and artificial hills |
| •SUGGESTED MAP• | aqua3 OS Explorer 160 Windsor, Weybridge & Bracknell |
| •START / FINISH• | Grid reference: TQ 058778 |
| •DOG FRIENDLINESS• | Not allowed in churchyard |
| •PARKING• | Limited parking in Harmondsworth village |
| •PUBLIC TOILETS• | By car park in Harmondsworth Moor |

## Walk 50 Directions

Turn right by the **Five Bells** pub into **Moor Lane** and follow this as it curves and narrows before coming to a bridge. Turn right into **Harmondsworth Moor** – an area of parkland that has been established by British Airways using 240 acres (97ha) of reclaimed land.

Harmondsworth Moor is the largest public park to be created in London for the past 100 years. It also boasts a Green Flag Award (for reaching certain standards set by the civic trusts). Surrounded by the M25 and the M4, and a little over 2 miles (3.2km) as the crow flies from Terminal 3, it's a wonder that such an attractive development could exist. True, you can hear the constant hum of traffic but the ubiquitous aircraft are hardly noticeable. It's easy to get your bearings as the award-winning British Airways Waterside office

complex and the adjacent Swan Lake are usually within sight. Ancient meadows have been recreated using specially harvested seeds, which in turn attract a range of insects, butterflies and birds. You'll discover some unique features, including part of Waterloo Bridge, amid these rolling hills and rivers. Wander through the park at will, or try the following route.

Take the right fork alongside the fence beside the **Duke of Northumberland's River** and

---

**WHERE TO EAT AND DRINK**

The **Five Bells** pub, with its low-beamed, cosy interior is welcoming. There are a couple of daily specials and an extensive menu includes sandwiches, jacket potatoes, pasta, pies and some Indian dishes such as chicken korma. Originally the village bakery, the pub is thought to be 300 years old. Avoid Friday lunchtimes if you want to be sure of a table because it can get busy with British Airways staff at that time.

Walk 50

continue, keeping to the right. Ahead is a mound, shaped like an amphitheatre, that faces a series of large granite and sandstone blocks. This is known as the **Giant's Teeth** and the blocks were part of the old Waterloo Bridge, before it was demolished in 1935.

### WHILE YOU'RE THERE ⓘ

If you have children with you and are walking during the week, call in at the **Community Learning Centre**, which offers an interactive wildlife experience for children of all ages. The centre works closely with the local residents. It holds workshops and has learning resources, including a mock interior of an aircraft, in which children can practise language and presentation skills. To find the centre, continue past Swan Lake instead of turning right to the car park.

Beside the Giant's Teeth is a raised, fenced area that you can enter through wooden gates and then follow a path to reach a suntrap with two benches. In summer the buddleia here attract plenty of butterflies. When you leave this area turn right, across a wooden bridge. Next, cross a footbridge, and go past a granite sculpture of a beetle standing on what was once an orchard, to go through the gate. Cross the road and go through a kissing gate. At the **Swan Lake**,

### WHAT TO LOOK FOR ⓘ

If you follow the path past Half Moon Meadow you will come to a **memorial** on the left. On 16th September 1948 a Royal Canadian Air Force Halifax bomber crashed here, killing all seven crew. The plaque is set in a block of stone – yes you've guessed it – from Waterloo Bridge, and every year British Airways and the village hold a small memorial service. The meadow is at its best in July and August when it is brightly coloured with poppies and corn marigolds.

which is adjacent to the Waterside office complex, turn right and follow this path through a gate a little further on the right. Cross the road into the car park and go through a gate on the far right. Turn left and follow a path towards a bridge over the **River Colne**. To your right here is **Half Moon Meadow**, a popular area for picnics. Turn left past the ponds. Take a right fork to reach the boardwalk over a pond and, after this, turn left to cross a footbridge. Go through a kissing gate and turn right to cross a bridge.

Turn right and then take the left-hand fork uphill to reach **The Keyhole**, where you'll see more stones from Waterloo Bridge. Also, you'll have a good view of the Wraysbury River ahead and the surrounding area. Notice the words of Alfred, Lord Tennyson that are aptly carved in the blocks: 'For words like nature half reveal and half conceal'.

Follow the path back down and take the left fork leading to a kissing gate and a bridge back over the Wraysbury River – this gravel-based river has a good supply of chub.

Turn left through the gate. At a fenced T-junction turn right and follow the path to a bridge over the northern part of the **Duke of Northumberland's River**. Turn right, signposted 'Harmondsworth', along a path that skirts the edge of **Saxon Lake**. At the far end go through the kissing gate and right along a narrow track, at the end of which is a metal gate leading to the churchyard. Mr Cox, of Cox's apples fame, is buried here. At the other end of this is the **Five Bells** pub, where your walk began.

# Walking in Safety

All these walks are suitable for any reasonably fit person, but less experienced walkers should try the easier walks first. Route finding is usually straightforward, but you will find that an Ordnance Survey map is a useful addition to the route maps and descriptions.

## Risks

Although each walk here has been researched with a view to minimising the risks to the walkers who follow its route, no walk in the countryside can be considered to be completely free from risk. Walking in the outdoors will always require a degree of common sense and judgement to ensure that it is as safe as possible.

- Be particularly careful on cliff paths and in upland terrain, where the consequences of a slip can be very serious.

- Remember to check tidal conditions before walking on the seashore.

- Some sections of route are by, or cross, busy roads. Take care and remember traffic is a danger even on minor country lanes.

- Be careful around farmyard machinery and livestock, especially if you have children with you.

- Be aware of the consequences of changes in the weather and check the forecast before you set out. Carry spare clothing and a torch if you are walking in the winter months. Remember the weather can change very quickly at any time of the year, and in moorland and heathland areas, mist and fog can make route finding much harder. Don't set out in these conditions unless you are confident of your navigation skills in poor visibility. In summer remember to take account of the heat and sun; wear a hat and carry spare water.

- On walks away from centres of population you should carry a whistle and survival bag. If you do have an accident requiring the emergency services, make a note of your position as accurately as possible and dial 999.

# Acknowledgements

Many people, both directly and indirectly, helped me during my research for this book. I would like to thank my family for their support and encouragement and also my friends: in particular Felicity Leicester, Carol Hooper, Revd Dr Martin Dudley of St Bartholomew the Great, Emma Dowson, Linda and Dee. Thanks also to rangers Dave Haldane and Roger Gates, and Mark from British Airways, David Bevan of Haringey environmental services, PC Richard Paterson of Wapping Marine Support, Simon Lee of the Lower Lea Project and Jennifer Curtin of Battersea Park. Acknowledgement must also go to the Countryside Agency, the Wildlife Trust and the dedicated individuals at the London boroughs who work in conjunction with the London Walking Forum to provide and maintain the footpaths.

AA Publishing and Outcrop Publishing Services would like to thank Chartech for supplying aqua3 maps for this book. For more information visit their website: www.aqua3.com.

**Series management:** Outcrop Publishing Services Ltd, Cumbria
**Series editor:** Chris Bagshaw
**Front cover:** AA Photo Library/Tim Woodcock